Peoria Winter

Peoria Winter

Styles and Resources in Later Life

John R. Kelly
University of Illinois

Lexington Books
D.C. Heath and Company/Lexington, Massachusetts/Toronto

Library of Congress Cataloging-in-Publication Data

Kelly, John R. (John Robert), 1930–
  Peoria winter.

  Includes index.
  1. Aged—Illinois—Peoria—Economic conditions—
Case studies. 2. Aged—Illinois—Peoria—Social
conditions—Case studies. 3. Life cycle, Human—
Case studies. I. Title.
HQ1064.U6I333 1987 305.2′6′0977352 86–45421
ISBN 0–669–13341–8 (alk. paper)

Published simultaneously in Canada
Printed in the United States of America
Casebound International Standard Book Number: 0–669–13341–8
Library of Congress Catalog Card Number: 86–45421

The paper used in this publication meets the minimum requirements
of American National Standard for Information Sciences—
Permanence of Paper for Printed Library Materials, ANSI
Z39.48–1984. ∞ ™

87 88 89 90 91 8 7 6 5 4 3 2 1

Contents

Figures and Tables

Figures

Tables

Preface

"Peoria winter" is a metaphor for the conditions of later life. Living in later-life years, as during the winter, can be difficult. Just as the cold makes car engines harder to start and the ice and snow make streets harder to negotiate, the cumulative effects of aging make life a little harder, calling for more effort in getting out, more care in getting around, and more planning in getting and staying involved in satisfying activities. After all, life at any age is more than bare functioning. We want to be engaged in satisfying activity and related to people whom we enjoy and for whom we care. Thus, later life is somewhat like winter in the personal and environmental difficulties that accumulate. Winter does not bring life to a halt, but it can make things more difficult.

The conditions of aging in Peoria are only the context for this study. First, we wanted to know more about the conditions of life as they are understood by those in the second half of the life course. Second, we wanted to know more about how "second-half" adults cope with those conditions. And, third, we were especially interested in the possible contributions of leisure to the coping processes.

The Life Course

The analytical framework for this study is the "life course." Life is a journey beginning with birth and ending with death. In between, we live through a series of events in company with others making their journeys. In the life course, there is a sequence of events that are relatively predictable. The transitions of student to worker to retiree and child to parent are made with others of about the same age, the "cohort" of those who parade together. However, individual life courses also have their "traumas" or life-altering events for which we seldom are prepared. The life course is characterized by change, both continuous and discontinuous, that calls for internal and external resources if we are to move on in a life that is satisfying.

The sequences of the life course do not unfold exactly alike for everyone. The succession of institutional roles is neither universal nor inevitable. All do not marry, have children, "launch" them from the home, and eventually become widowed or leave a spouse alone. Most adults seem to have a series of jobs rather than an orderly and progressive work "career." In fact, most of the Peoria adults studied intensively experienced at least one major trauma in their journeys to the present. Nevertheless, the life course—regular or problematic—remains a useful framework from which to analyze both the continuities and discontinuities of life for second-half adults.

Coping with Change

Everyone has to cope with life course change. No two life journeys, however, are just alike. We can hardly expect, then, that the methods and strategies of coping will be alike either. The personal resources that we develop are not likely to be quite like those of anyone else, regardless of socioeconomic categories or any other means of classification. While the external or social resources available to us may be more generalizable by, for example, gender or social class, those we employ will usually form a combination unique to our histories.

We did find that social placement factors such as education level, family structure, and employment history provide common limitations on perceived and used resources. The continuities, however, were more striking for individuals than categories. Even allowing for the process of enhancing the appearance of consistency by "making sense" of the recollected past, the behavior described by 120 later-life adults seemed to demonstrate consistent patterns of coping. By the time they are 40 or 60 or 80 years old, individuals have developed characteristic styles of dealing with change. It is those styles that we will use in the first part of this book to try to understand the complex realities of the later life course.

Further, we will focus on the social dimension of intimate community. In the past, social gerontologists have done considerable research on "helpers," "caretakers," and helping networks. We will alter the focus somewhat to look at those with whom older persons share their life course sequences. Finally, we will attempt to reanalyze the meaning of "success" in coping with later-life changes.

Certainties and Uncertainties

Most persons experience parental nurture, school, employment, the formation of one or more new-family households, the death of significant others, and some phased withdrawal from the labor force. These "likelihoods" may be out of sequence, off time, interrupted, repeated, or otherwise different from the normative order. Nevertheless, such a life-course framework offers expectations that most people either fulfill or from which they deviate by choice or necessity.

Such likelihoods can usually be anticipated with mental and logistical preparation easing the transitions. On the other hand, the certainty of uncertainty calls for a different kind of response. Coping with unexpected change that may disrupt the "normal" sequence of roles and transitions may be disintegrating. The contexts, resources, abilities, associations, and requirements of life may be radically altered by a trauma. Coping may be quite singular as an individual has to cope with change being experienced by no one else in one's immediate circle of intimates. The support of going through a transition with others is absent. As a consequence, the development of resources and resilience are also singular in the story of each person.

The collaborative interviews are one means of investigating this singularity. In them, individuals "tell their stories." And they also tell what that personal history "means" to them, how they understand the events. Although each story is unique, there are also commonalities. In the 120 stories, patterns emerge that lead to the development of typologies of coping: characteristic styles of moving through the life course. These styles are related to two main factors: available resources and personal orientations.

The Research Base

In a project funded by the National Institute on Aging (PH 5 R01 AG02933-01,02), we went to that prototypical community of Peoria, Illinois, to complete a research sequence. The strategy was to begin with a general community sample of 400 adults, age 40 and over. Employing telephone interviews, we obtained information about their family, work, community, and leisure roles and engagements. These interviews provided a kind of map of the territory, indicating where our subjects were in their community contexts and life-course roles.

However, viewing the life course in a processual way and believing that how people define themselves and their worlds is crucial to understanding any aspect of their lives, we then selected 120 of the 400 for face-to-face interviews. The mode of the second wave of interviews was that of "collaboration" in which they were asked to join with the interviewer and others on the research team in interpreting their lives. The interviews had a general framework in which changes in the work, family, and leisure domains of life were discussed with particular attention given to intersections between domains and resources from one that carried over into others.

Finally, near the end of the two-year period that had begun in the spring of 1983, we completed a mail survey of the 400 that included some scales measuring life orientations or investments, patterns of leisure meaning and satisfaction, and items checking the reliability of elements of the previous data.

The age frame, beginning with age 40, was selected because the final or "culminating" period of the life course begins whenever individuals begin to recognize that their span of years has limits. This recognition is often accompanied by the inauguration of a process of "making sense" of life, both past and future. Our hope was to meet people in various stages of this process and utilize the insights that they were developing. However, premises that guided our research design include the following:

> Men and women may define themselves differently as well as have access to different resources. Therefore, the sample as well as the interview formats should be sensitive to the gender factor.

> Age is not a factor itself, but does index common changes in the life course. Therefore, age groupings need to reflect the full range of the second-half life course.

> Other critical factors in coping are more problematic. Level of education, however, not only indexes resources, but also is a less gender-biased criterion for sample selection than occupation. Further, cohort differences in mean education level make this a crucial variable for examining historical change.

> Marital and family status and history are also central to every other aspect of the life course.

Also, while the cooperation of our subjects was entirely voluntary and no concealment was employed, we have protected their privacy by separating identifying codes from the interview data and by altering the case study material enough to obscure identification. We are so grateful to those who joined in this process of research that we could do no less to protect them, regardless of regulation.

A Note on Validity and Reliability

Some would argue that the research issues of validity and reliability are not applicable to the kind of research that underlies this presentation. However, if validity is an assurance that our data have some real correspondence with the lives of our subjects, we would ask critics to listen to a few of our taped interviews and compare them with the telephone and mail studies of the same persons. Certainly the data are recollective and filtered through years of self-interpretation. But both consistency from one data format to another and the persuasive authenticity within the interviews suggests that although we may not have the whole story for anyone, what we do have is remarkably close to their interpretation of real events.

While we also attempted to support reliability by employing the interpretations of at least three research team members for each subject and by comparing data items between telephone and face-to-face interviews, there is no way of demonstrating that all inconsistencies are identified or eliminated. Perhaps the strongest evidence of reliability is the coherence of the material available on each subject. Sometimes as trust and communication increased interviews produced surprises. However, in general, the pictures of each person developed in ways that enhanced but did not contradict previous material. Although reworking by a different team might refine details and realign emphases, we believe that the overall interpretations would usually stand up to replication.

This confidence leads me to acknowledge the work of other members of the research team. First is the dedicated and always competent work of Marjorie W. Steinkamp, Project Coordinator, who was at the center of everything. From drawing samples to analyzing data and profiles, she contributed integrally to every aspect of the project. Telephone interviewing was conducted largely and extremely well by Ann Willig, with the assistance of Jan Sneegas and John Datillo. The collaborative interviews were conducted by Jim Klein, Laura Lee, Keith Savell, Sylvia Sparkis, and Jan Sneegas, who were graduate students at the time of the study. Janice Kelly set up the computerized data files and ran analyses of the telephone interview data and the mail survey. Laura Lee also managed the mini-computer files and completed further analysis. Professor Martin L. Maehr contributed early advice and participated in the team meetings during the collaborative interview stage. In all, we were a "team" in the best sense of the term with contributions so interwoven that the mutual support, corrections, and insights can never be allocated to individuals. Finally, I appreciate the helpful criticism and corrections offered by Jan Sneegas and Marjorie Steinkamp who read the entire manuscript and contributed to any strengths the reader may find. I am grateful to all for what they did and for the experience of working with them.

Peoria Winter

1
The Later-Life Course

The journey of life is singular. No two life journeys are alike, and no one story can represent the experience of all men or women of our time. Yet there are commonalities. We chose to focus on the people of Peoria because this Midwestern city is rated an exceptional place for test marketing. Its population distributions are close to the national averages of age, income, occupational levels, education, and other such indices. However, no one would argue that lives in Peoria represent those of the rest of the country. Silicon Valley it is not. Yet, the people of Peoria do represent most of the fundamental experiences of the life course. Their opportunities, barriers, successes, losses, and even evaluations are much like those of people elsewhere. They cope with birth and death, routine and surprise, pain and joy. They are tied to others and yet often alone, enriched by others and yet caught in webs of frustration, believing in significant others and yet sometimes betrayed. In coming to know even a few of our collaborators in Peoria, we have come to know something of everyone's journey and of the social fabric of any community.

Two Life Journeys: Coping with Change

It would be convenient if we could find among the 120 persons whom we interviewed intensively one individual whose life seemed to sum up the critical changes and coping patterns for the entire sample. But no such prototype emerged. There are persistent themes, definable patterns, and common problems. But we found that each man and woman who was interviewed emerged as an individual. We identified three types of life courses and nine styles of coping related to resources and life orientations. However, the people we listened to as they recounted their adult life courses and interpreted their meaning were far more than types. Meet two of them in enough detail to get a sense of the richness of their accounts. (Individuals have been given different names to protect their privacy.)

Nat and the Household of Children

Nat's life seemed to be a natural unfolding of cumulative relationships that gave focus and direction to his life course. Nat is a retired deputy sheriff who gained considerable satisfaction from the "helping mode" in which he defined his work role. Even now there are those who greet him in a store or restaurant and remind him that he is "known" and remembered. That is no small accomplishment for a black man in an industrial city with 95% of its quarter million population white. He gained considerable satisfaction in a job requiring that he respond to crisis in the lives of others. Listening to his stories, you accept that his eighth-grade education level was no real impediment to his competence.

However, the center of Nat's life was not work. It was, and is, family. He defines the context and the meaning of his life in terms of the four-generation extended family, many of whom still live either in the grandparental home or within a few blocks. He is "family-focused" in the sense that his life is defined primarily by his investment in those intimate others. He describes his home as "a household of children" with grandchildren still living with him and his wife. Sons and daughters live within a few blocks. The house in which they have lived for 35 years is not a possession or financial investment, but a place for family. Holidays were family. "If the kids couldn't go, we didn't go either." The family theme is so pervasive that the world is defined by it. Financial help, emotional support, and self-definition are found in that world. Nat's family is not so much "extended" as integrated.

Of course there were problems. In 50 years of marriage, Nat and his wife could always sit down and talk things out. Since "nothing serious" happened, they never had to seek "outside" help. The impression is one of such mutual commitment that the sharing of both joy and pain was as much the atmosphere of life as air.

Nat's life course has not been a planned excursion as much as a ramble through the countryside with an ever-increasing number of intimates. Where does he feel most free to be himself? With family and friends, especially when travelling. When is he most likely to feel good about himself? In the process of "keeping the family together" and in "assisting other people with their problems." In this sense of community, Nat never made big future plans, but "lived day by day." Recall that he was for years the black deputy—a minority in what is usually considered a high stress occupation. His children and grandchildren experienced the multiple forms of discrimination and personal traumas in the years before, during, and after the Civil Rights movement. Yet, this thoughtful and intelligent man took it all a day at a time.

The focus on the family does not mean that Nat has no other satisfactions or investments. He goes to Alaska for fishing with friends. He enjoys the competition of an occasional card game. He buys old cars and rebuilds them as a challenge to his skills. However, even in his leisure, family comes first. The activity he would be most reluctant to surrender would be visiting family and friends. His son comes over three or four times a week, and they "put on the coffee pot." He enjoys the companionship, but cannot separate that from the value he places on strengthening the relationship. His second most important leisure activity is travel, both Caribbean cruises with his wife and long auto trips. He finds travel exciting, healthy, and a relaxing change as well as a context for companionship. And, in Alaska he will fish until his arms are tired when he is caught up in the excitement and the healthy environment.

He thinks that public programs for other retired people are just for "people who are lost." He has never been to a senior center and has all the stereotypes in mind as he describes why "sitting around playing cards and exchanging lies" would never interest him. He cannot imagine a time when he would be bereft of companions or of things he wanted to do.

Nat enjoys travel and is willing to invest time and money in opportunities for such expression. He remembers his work with the satisfaction that he helped others and received some personal recognition for what he was able to do. His leisure and work cannot be seen as strictly instrumental with family providing the real purpose for everything else. Yet, the dominant color of his life tapestry is familial. In this context, he feels fulfilled and worthwhile.

Nat's life course was quite regular without any major traumas requiring responses that rearranged his values or his social situation. However, such a regular life course characterized a minority of those whom we interviewed. More common were those who had one major "turning point" requiring major life-changing response or who had a series of events producing a "zigzag" journey. Mary is one of those who has had to cope with a series of traumas that we might have considered extraordinary before engaging the lives of so many who did not find smooth sailing in their lives.

Making It—Mary's Multiple Investments

Things are much better now for 62–year-old Mary. However, her life journey has had many sharp twists and turns. A bare outline suggests the strenuous requirements for coping.

Her first marriage ended in divorce. She filed for divorce from her husband who had been institutionalized in a mental hospital for ten years only after learning that his consistent evening absences had been due to involvement with other women.

Her second marriage continued through 15 stormy years. As her husband's alcoholism developed, she found some help in Al-Anon only to discover that he was skipping Alcoholics Anonymous to go out drinking. Finally, his physical abuse of both her and their daughter forced her to sever the relationship.

Her employment career has also zigzagged as family need and priorities changed. At times she did laundry and sewing for others to augment the family income. During her first marriage, she did house cleaning. Now at age 62 she is working in an office—mostly with women younger than her children. She began this job ten years ago when she realized that a second divorce was imminent and that she would have to be self-supporting.

Mary has three adult children, the youngest of whom was married only two years ago. Her childhood as one of ten in her family was a Depression-era situation. She left school after ten years and was able to return only for a few night business courses years later. Yet, she is very calm and articulate. She believes that her life conditions have improved dramatically. Her work companions like and respect her. Most important, "I have three wonderful children." Considering the marriage history, she feels justified in taking pride in that. All in all, despite the history of insecurity and hardship, she now has a balanced and structured life that she finds satisfying. Just what are the components of that balance?

Mary can be termed a "balanced investor" because of the way in which she finds meaning and satisfaction in her work, family, and leisure. She has been told at the printing business that the office couldn't run without her. That's quite a boost in her sense of self-worth. For a woman who experienced "being put down quite a bit by two husbands, that helps." From cleaning houses and Aid for Families with Dependent Children to valued employee of a business with a national clientele is no small feat.

The second dimension of her balance is her children. Even now that they are married and independent, she takes great pride in bringing them through all the difficulties. She knows her eldest son would be ready to help her if needed, but tends to view the future in a spirit of self-reliance.

The third dimension is leisure. "I cannot conceive of a time when I would not be doing things," she adds to an account of her adult leisure history. She enjoys other people, but has also learned to be alone. "I have spent most of my life by myself," she reflects on thinking of the lack of marital companionship. Perhaps that is why she has developed a full set of leisure engagements.

Religious participation is important in providing an opportunity for growth, helping others, and belonging to a stable community. She enjoys informal interaction with family and friends and sees the value of enhancing and expressing those relationships. She really lights up, however, when she describes the Quadrant Club and its dance program. The club is for adult singles only and brings together a group of men and women who like dancing. "I learned to dance when I was in my 30s and never stopped." Most of her nonwork friends are in that club. Sometimes they even charter a bus and go to the Chicago area for a supplement to their own once-a-week dance.

She watches TV "a lot, more than I want to." When she retires, she may begin again to sew costumes for a local theatre group. She had enjoyed it, but hasn't had time in recent years. She gave up bowling because some of the women were "crude." "Bellyflopping on a sled" had been fun, but didn't seem appropriate after the years piled up. It's the dance club where she now feels most natural and free.

And, then, there is Helen. Helen is her best friend. They have been through a lot together—divorce, rebuilding a life, and the support of a church-based group. They talk almost every evening as well as go to the dance group and eat out together. They share intimately and fully because they have such similar life courses. The leisure contexts provide times and places for such sharing. Now, along with other dance companions, they make their way though preretirement years together and deal with the consequences of aging in supporting company.

With such a zigzag life course, Mary gives only fleeting notice to some of the kind of events that others might find staggering. By the age of 39 she had major surgery three times. Altogether she has undergone surgery "eight or nine times." She sees such health events as "just another problem in life."

Yes, life is better now. Mary has the satisfaction of her adult children, work where she is valued, communication and sharing with one close friend and other regular associations, and as much activity as she can accommodate. She may have been alone emotionally for much of her life; but now when she is actually living alone, she feels more a part of communities. She has not just let life push her around. She has sought and found investments that have paid off in bringing balance and texture to her life. Somehow, all the context-destroying events have not taken from her the self-acceptance and direction required to go on forming relationships that offer a sharing of both meaning and joy.

Nat and Mary are only two cases, two people whose life stories are each remarkable and yet are certainly not the most dramatic among our 120 collaborators. Nat's life course was relatively smooth and satisfying despite being black in a time and place of racial discrimination and turmoil. Mary's life has been characterized by the betrayal and failure of others as well as by economic deprivation and health setbacks. Yet, she has overcome so much that her quiet story becomes one of great resilience and unspoken determination. Neither has had much in the way of the resources so popular in the literature on midlife "passages" or the development of "human potential." No professional counselor gave critical insight or life-changing renewal, although Mary did receive significant strength from a Catholic sharing group. They are not very glamourous people and live in an environment infamous for being ordinary. Yet, they are special in demonstrating the potential for life-developing decisions and attachments that are common to so many of those whom we came to know.

Elements of Analysis

The life-course framework begins with the premise that life is processual. Each life journey is both cumulative and disjunctive, predictable and problematic. Further, each individual makes the journey in a particular historical epoch, a specific social and cultural context, and with a matrix of interrelationships that have their own complex stories. At any moment in the process, we are what we have become and at the same time we are still "becoming." There is no time or place in which the process is fixed and can be investigated in a changefree mode.

Nevertheless, there are a number of interrelated dimensions that are common to all life journeys even when their relative influence varies from person to person. Before going on to the presentation of our analysis of later life in Peoria, these dimensions should be identified. They are not "concrete facts" or mathematically constructed theories of clear cause and effect. Rather, they may be viewed as metaphors or perspectives that have been found to yield important understanding of the kind of phenomena we are studying (Kelly, 1986). They are neither exhaustive nor fully determinative. Together, however, they seem to draw in the most useful elements of explanation related to our field of study—change and coping in the second half of the life course.

The life course has already been introduced. Its beginning-to-end structure provides a framework for dealing with both continuity and change. It highlights demonstrated commonalities in the lives of those who make their life journeys in similar times and places without forcing individual differences into a binding mold (Riley, 1979).

Age is used here as an index rather than a force. While it is true that a number of changes in life are correlated with advancing age, there is no universality or inevitability that is age-exact. Tendencies toward diminution of strength and endurance vary widely. Role losses in work and family settings may be gradual, sudden, or be reversed by taking on new ties and responsibilities. Health changes and trajectories vary. And even the inevitable end of death occurs for individuals with massive disregard for actuarial tables. Age, however, remains a useful index of probabilities (George, 1980). In this study age categories are employed to describe tendencies toward personal and contextual change, but not to suggest inevitable age-linked rates or sequences.

Life domains are the major identifiable sectors of life in which we invest ourselves and from which we anticipate positive outcomes. For adults in our culture, the three domains of work, family, and leisure tend to be most salient. The rewards of the work domain include market power (income), social standing or place, and the possibility of a sense of productivity or social contribution. If "family" is defined broadly to include communities of committed relationship, nurture, and a history of common residence as well as the sanctioned marriage, then it provides companionship, security, many dimensions of regular sharing, and a sense of belonging. When "leisure" is understood as activity chosen rather than required and with a central element of being done for its own sake, for the experience, then it encompasses activity in which selfhood and community are developed and expressed (Kelly, 1983). All three life domains have points of intersection that shift through the life course. They are not discrete; they are woven together in resources, associations, and meanings.

Social institutions include the economic and family domains as well as political, religious, educational, and voluntary organizations with norms and aims consistent enough to be metaphorically termed "structure." These institutions are said to be functionally interrelated in ways that together carry out those tasks necessary for the continuation of the social system. Each institutional domain is composed of "roles" in which regular behavioral expectations are integrated to enable the institution to carry out its social functions. From an interpretive perspective, individuals take those roles in ways that express some individuality rather than simply conform to clear and complete norms. That is, they tend to "play" roles rather than become them (Kelly, 1983).

Stratification is the division of members of a social system into persistent segments with differential access to resources and power. In most analyses, such stratification is presumed to be based on economic roles and opportunities. Further, the differential access to resources is a major factor in what is possible through the entire life course (Sennett and Cobb, 1972). "Social class" refers to the differential opportunities in life that are based on economic position and consequent political leverage. "Social status" refers to the evaluated modes of life and social access that are outcomes of being born and raised in a social class.

Coping refers to the means by which a person or group responds to an event or circumstance in order to survive or overcome its consequences. Coping may include rebellion and counterattack as well as "adaptation," in which the change is largely on the part of the individual experiencing the external force. The variety of coping behaviors tends to follow from how the circumstance and the self are defined as well as differences in the resources seen as available.

Investments are the choices made by persons or groups that embody longer-term commitments of self and resources. The premise is that there is an existential thrust to many decisions that contain the expectation or hope of positive returns on the investment. Such investments may be made in any life domain.

The Research Process

The dilemma of social research is that life will not stand still to be examined. Every social act is a process in which there is some element of the problematic. In every act, there is some development of the self, some learning, however minute and immeasurable. Even the most brief and trivial episodes involve changes in moods and feelings as well as in definitions of the situation. While most such change may be trivial, it remains the case that there is no moment that necessarily epitomizes the process.

How much more is this true of the process of coping with the institutionalization of a mentally ill husband or assisting a grandchild whose marriage is dissolving? How can the satisfactions of a close friendship or a two-week trip to Alaska be summarized in the ranking of statements or the completion of a scale? While the intensive interview in which stories are told and feelings expressed may seem more responsive to significant life course processes, even in this mode the subject is being asked to select themes, illustrative moments, and general interpretations from a complex history. There is no single method that does it all.

For this reason, the research strategy adopted to investigate later-life coping processes among Peoria adults incorporates several approaches. The method is both sequential and cumulative. The collaborative interviews were from the beginning assumed to be the center of the sequence. Every step, however, had its own integrity as well as the promise of contributing to the overall enterprise. The sequence consisted of three waves of obtaining data. Each built on the previous stage, but was subjected to separate as well as comparative analysis.

Peoria is a river town in central Illinois that has been used as a market research site because of its relative media isolation as well as demographic profile. In age, education level, occupational classification, and income, Peoria is within 2 to 4 percent of national distributions. It has a private university and community college, a modest new civic center, a decaying downtown and lavish peripheral shopping centers, a hospital complex, a variety of industries including the international leader in construction machinery, Peoria Caterpillar. During the period of the research, 1983–85, an economic recession had raised unemployment levels to record highs and forced many workers to face the specter of structural unemployment. This does not make Peoria different, but highlights conditions common to many communities. "How it plays in Peoria" may not represent every political, social, and economic facet of American life, but will do about as well as any other single community.

Stage 1: The Telephone Interviews. From a current telephone directory, a sample was chosen using a table of random numbers so that every listing had an equal chance of selection. The aim was to complete 400 interviews with adults age 40 and older. Every number was called repeatedly at various times of the day and evening with call-backs made if someone 40 years or older was in residence but not available. Refusal rate was 32% of the total. The sample turned out to be 66% female, 30% over 64, 61% with high school education or less, and 48% currently employed. All distributions were representative of the community for their age cohorts.

The interviews were 15 minutes in length to maximize the chances of a willingness to participate in the subsequent face-to-face sessions. The instrument included demographic items, range and frequency of leisure activity, a brief life-satisfaction scale, measures of perceived problems such as health and income, and the scope and frequency of social interaction. We wanted to know about problems such as lack of friends, health, loneliness, boredom, inadequate housing, and lack of income that might affect other aspects of life. The subjects provided a frequency estimate for 28 kinds of leisure activity that had been found in previous research to be most common for older adults and a satisfaction scale for those two activities considered most important to them. When 10 items as well as this scale were repeated in the later interviews six to ten months later, there was 96 percent agreement.

Many kinds of statistical analysis were employed and have been reported in articles in journals specializing in social gerontology and leisure studies (Kelly et al., 1986a,b, 1987; Steinkamp and Kelly, 1986a,b). The main purpose was to measure the independent contributions of leisure to social integration and overall life satisfaction when health, marital status, age, education level, gender, and occupation level were taken into account. One surprise, to be examined in chapter 7, was that the level of leisure activity was found to make more of a difference in life satisfaction than any other factor.

Stage 2: The Collaborative Interviews. The real heart of the research, however, was the face-to-face interviews conducted with 120 of those who had participated in the telephone interviews. So much research on older people has used subjects with some special institutional relationship—program participants, church members, or those in a health-care facility—that we wanted to avoid that bias. So, the telephone sample became the basis for the selection of second-wave participants. The selection was not random. Rather, four factors were found in the stage one analysis to be most salient to coping: age, gender, marital status, and education level. For example, we interviewed two of the three married males age 75 and over, but not half of the 30 married males age 40 to 54. We sought a sample that represented the conditions of aging rather than a statistical sample.

The interviews were conducted by the research team; two faculty and five graduate students from the University of Illinois at Urbana-Champaign. The interviews lasted from 45 minutes to well over two hours. The outline followed the general format of asking about major changes in work, family, and health since age 40 and how the subject had coped with them. Just who had helped, if anyone, and the nature of the relationships were probed. There were questions about continuities and changes in leisure and how leisure was related to work and family. The salience of personal and social resources as well as styles of response to both transitions and traumas were approached in several ways.

Interviews were tape-recorded and interviewers took notes on impressions and interpretations. Within 48 hours after the interview, the interviewer was to complete a structured "profile" that summarized the main issues in a computerized file that was coded for cross-referencing. The profile printouts as well as the tapes provide records that can be used repeatedly in the interpretation process. During the six months of interviewing, the team met weekly to discuss problems and exchange insights.

Further, immediate feedback and support was available during the shared 1½ hour drives back after morning and afternoon interviews.

The central data, then, were focused interviews in which the subjects were asked to participate in the interpretation process. There was no concealment of aims or instruments. Rather, they joined, sometimes with great enthusiasm and insight, into the attempt to understand the events and meanings of their adult life courses.

Stage 3: The Mailed Follow-up. In the summer of 1984, the original 400 were mailed a questionnaire that included a number of scales. Two scales measured self-assessment of "social competence." One was a measure of the kinds of satisfactions and meaning found in leisure in general, another a fuller replication of the Life Satisfaction Index (LSI), and the third a scale on "life investments" or orientations developed by members of the team. By then some in the sample had died, moved, or were unable to complete such instruments. However, 217 usable returns provided a third kind of information.

The Classification Scheme

Perhaps the most controversial element of the analysis and interpretation of all this material is the two classification schemes that were developed. Case study research has a long history of the use of such "typologies" to attempt to find and report consistencies from one case to another. Even recognizing that no individual exactly fits the definition of any type, the method provides one way of organizing the rich and complex findings in a way that they can be comprehended by those who have not scanned all the hundreds of pages of computer printouts and listened to the hundreds of hours of interviews.

The historical justification for the method is found in the work of one of the "fathers" of modern sociology, Max Weber. Weber believed that explaining human action and interaction required engaging in an interpretive process that used the powers of imaginative thought to enter the thoughts of others. This *verstehen* process was to be self-critical and reflexive (Weber, 1946). Rather than seek a mathematical precision that could be repeated, social research was in each case a unique act that attempted to make sense of related actions that were precisely unrepeatable. However, the continuities and commonalities of similar actions might be analyzed by identifying the common dimensions and constructing "ideal types" that brought those dimensions into clear focus.

The typologies developed out of the collaborative interviews are ideal types, constructions based on the life-course stories and particular dimensions of coping with change. The process of development was self-critical as well as interpretive. From the interviews, three clear kinds of life courses were identified on the basis of the severity and number of traumatic events requiring major changes to cope with them. The types of response patterns were more varied. Four main kinds of coping styles characterized about 80% of the sample. Two were based on "investments" and resources, and two were more psychological in nature. However, five other ideal types were also identified and employed in the analysis—partly as contrasting alternatives and partly because they might be expected by persons who believe previous stereotypes of explanation. The classifications were done by the two senior investigators independently and then compared. In the 30% of cases where there were disagreements, discussion inevitably revealed that the differences were a matter of the weight given particular behaviors and statements. The final classifications were assigned only when consensus was reached in a reexamination of the interview and profile materials.

The Life-Course Types

1. *Straight Arrow* (SA) (40%): SAs had a life course that proceeded with the predictable adult transitions of launching children, employment shifts, and retirement. There was no major disruption. The transitions could be anticipated and handled with the support of others in their cohort dealing with the same on-time changes.

2. *Turning Point* (TP) (23%): A single event redirected the remainder of a TP's life course. Major personal and social adaptation was required. Such events included the early death or incapacitating illness of a spouse, incapacitating mental or physical illness of the subject, alcoholism, divorce for a family-centered person, and catastrophic economic loss.

3. *Zigzag* (ZZ) (37%): ZZs had two or more events that required significant change. Such a life course might have several stops and restarts, especially when a low level of economic resources compound the impacts of health loss or other trauma.

Note that 60% of the subsample of the 120 who engaged in the intensive interviews had turning point or zigzag life courses. A journey in which the changes can be anticipated and made in company with others who are on schedule was, at least for this sample, the minority pattern. Unexpected and powerful events had struck most of the sample. Somewhat surprisingly, there was no significant relationship between age and life-course type except for those over 75 years old who were only half as likely as the rest of the sample to be SAs and 50% more likely to be ZZs. There were also no gender differences or any relationship between occupational level and life-course disruptions. The pattern of relationship between education level and life-course type had only one consistent pattern: those with less than a high school education were disproportionately TPs who had experienced a major life-altering event. Often those who leave school early have had disrupting events. However, in general, the Psalmist's claim that "the rain falls on the just and unjust alike" seems to apply as well to life conditions. Traumas are about as likely to be experienced by men as women, by those of high as low social status, and by those with greater as lesser resources. The only exception is found among those who have outlived many of their intimates and are facing severe health problems in their last years of life.

Nat's life course was remarkably regular. He, then, is a classic SA with no major traumas. Mary, on the other hand, experienced the multiple disruptions of the ZZ type. The three life-course types provide a useful way of classifying the change conditions of our interviewees. The focus of the study, however, has been on the patterns of coping. Again, although no two individuals tell stories that are alike, the means of coping have dominant themes.

Styles of Coping

In the process of assigning descriptive labels to the coping strategies of those who engaged in the collaborative interviews, the initial idea was to categorize on a single dimension. The assumption was that individuals would concentrate on particular life domains in locating resources for support. Work, family, religion, community organizations, and leisure would offer the resources for rebuilding personal and social lives after a disruptive event or in a severely limiting condition. However, the approach of "grounded theory" (Glaser and Strauss, 1967) does not permit research analysts to force their preconceptions on those they study.

Several formats of classification were tried. One offered a three-step sequence of analysis: from type of life course to adaptation success or failure employing designated sources of help to use of leisure for social or personal renewal. A more psychological scheme began with three patterns of response: accepting, fighting, and experiencing no challenge or threat. However, after the three life-course types were adopted, the patterns of response, especially for TPs and ZZs, seemed more complex than could be encompassed by these earlier models.

Two alterations had to be made in the original scheme. The first required the addition of a second dimension. Where resources were found was one major theme. However, a significant number of adults were found to have styles of coping that could be termed internal rather than external. The primary dimension of their style was personal rather than social. They tended either to be quite self-sufficient or to have a relatively passive pattern of acceptance. Further, we found these styles were more likely to characterize women than men.

The second alteration also required the creation of a new category. Many of the subjects, often those who had seemed to cope with trauma most successfully, did not concentrate on a single life domain. Rather, they were deeply invested in at least two domains of work, family, leisure, and voluntary organizations. Like Mary, they had achieved some balance in their lives and could not fairly be forced into a category that stressed only one source of support and one domain of investment. Once the initial analysis scheme was revised on the basis of discussions among members of the research team, the classification process proceeded with relatively easy arrival at consensus.

Nine Types of Coping

1. Balanced Investors (40%): The largest single category was added to the scheme of "ideal types" when so many subjects just could not be placed into a category that specified one dominant life domain that provided most resources for coping with change. Just as important, these individuals had made positive decisions to invest themselves in at least two central life domains. For most, the family was a major source of meaning and satisfaction. However central this commitment and locus of meaningful integration (Gordon et al., 1976), they had clearly sought and achieved a balance with salient investment in work, leisure, or a voluntary organization, or all three, as well. While the most common balance was between economic and family roles, special engagements with religion, political action, the arts, travel, or some other form of activity were also integral to the commitment patterns of many balanced investors. Balanced investors were slightly more likely than the entire sample to be at the highest life-satisfaction level. They were disproportionately in professional and managerial occupations and most likely to have had some college education. Twenty five of the 48 balanced investors were male, the 52–48% ratio considerably higher than the 40–60% division of the sample. However, like Mary, 16 of the 48 had a high school education or less.

2. Family-Focused (19%): Those whose investments and support were found predominately in the family made up the next largest category. Like Nat, they simply cannot talk about their lives apart from the family, both as the locus of meaningful community and of personal investment. Both major and daily decisions are made with the consequences for the family foremost. Even after their children have begun their own families, the ties are strong. Especially when traumas occur, it is family who provide major emotional support, counsel, and often direct assistance. Work is defined as largely instrumental even when it provides enjoyable companions and some social identity. Leisure is for and with the family. Family-focused subjects were slightly more likely to be at the highest level of life satisfaction than balanced investors with only 5 of the 23 at low levels. The family-focused were disproportionately in the preretirement-age groups and have clerical, industrial, or sales jobs. The sex ratio was 44–56%, slightly more male than the sample. However, the family-focused were almost twice as likely as the sample to have no college education with only 5 of the 23 having any college at all and only one with any graduate education.

3. Work-Centered (3%): The ideal type of work-centered adults is certainly a theoretical possibility in a culture said to be permeated by a work ethic. However, only four individuals were found to invest themselves so fully in the economic sphere that the remainder of life was only a complement to this central identity-providing role. Surprisingly, three of the four were women. However, it was not a surprise that three of the four were in the professional, managerial, and self-employed occupational groups. One of the four, an unskilled worker, was extremely low in life satisfaction, and two were high.

4. Leisure-Invested (3%): In a preformed typology, the possibility that some might define their life meaning and important relationships in one or more leisure investments balanced the work-centered possibility. They did balance—in their infrequency. The four leisure-invested subjects were below average in life satisfaction. Three were preretirement in age, three female, and only one in a technical–professional occupation calling for college education.

5. Faithful Members (4%): In terms of both social resources in coping with change as well as centrality in interpreting life, only five focused on a non-familial community. The church was central to four individuals, one a retired Protestant pastor and one the widow of a minister. Faithful members were average or above average in life satisfaction, in unskilled occupations or retired, and without college education. Three were women, and three over the age of 75.

6. The Self-Sufficient (12%): Fifteen persons had developed consistent patterns of self-reliance in coping with change. Married or not, they found their resources within themselves, turned to no one else for advice or necessary support, and were not deeply engaged in any work or leisure roles. In each case, probes from somewhat skeptical interviewers elicited responses consistent with the self-definition of essential self-sufficiency. Most were either in relationships that were limited in communication richness or had lived alone in early adulthood. The self-sufficients were varied in life satisfaction. They were somewhat overrepresented in the higher occupational categories, about average in education with 7 of the 15 having attended college, and in the older age categories. Five of the 15 were age 75 or over. All but two were women.

7. Accepting Adaptors (12%): There were also 15 subjects in the second type based on personal characteristics rather than social resources. Accepting adaptors just seem to take whatever life has to offer. They change their own lives as necessary. They are passive rather than active and seldom attempt to alter the circumstances of their lives. Often with a clear or implicit religious philosophy, they believe that accepting and going on is what life is all about. They expect little help and take no direct action that will place them in a different context or develop new resources. Eighty percent—12 of the 15—were women. Only three had attended college at all and none had a degree. They were in service and low-skill occupations and were distributed five each in the 55-64, 65-74, and 75+ age categories. Only two were high in life satisfaction. They were twice the overall ratio in the lowest satisfaction levels.

8. Resistant Rebels (2%): Only two subjects—both were men—were classified as resisters. They believed that they had been treated unfairly by the social system or some immediate aspect of the system. Their response was anger and some attempt to change their environment. While the ideal type would suggest political militancy, the individuals were likely to be labelled as maladjusted by neighbors and to live in relative isolation. Low in educational background and occupational status, their anger seemed to reflect their marginal position more than any philosophy or ideology. As might be expected, they were quite low in life satisfaction.

9. Diffuse Dabblers (3%): Four in the sample had no consistent or persistent life investments. Nor did they demonstrate a high level of inner resources for coping. Rather, they seemed to wander aimlessly from one unsatisfying relationship and role to another. Although one was high and two average in life satisfaction, they had not made central investments that carried through the adult life course. Three of the four had low education and occupation levels.

The distributions are given only in relation to the overall distributions and in general terms because the sample size precludes identifying more than major tendencies. Further, reliance on averages would obscure important variations within each category. For example, one diffuse dabbler is a professional with a graduate education and a high level of life satisfaction. While accepting adaptors tend to be below the mean for life satisfaction, two have found this mode of coping to be highly satisfactory. We may learn as much from those who deviate from the type in a significant way as from those who are more average. Therefore, in the next five chapters, we will be examining the cases in each type in more detail.

Typologies and Life-Course Analysis

A significant analytical dilemma of any social research is trying to measure a process with static indicators. One solution is to follow a sample over time in a longitudinal design that can encompass history. However, even this solution compares two or more static measures rather than keeps contact with the process itself. Recently, complex statistical methods have been employed to measure indices of change for samples large enough that confounding variables can be measured and separated from those central to the analysis.

The dilemma remains, whether the "slicing" measures are obtained once or several times. The actual course of the process is not encompassed by even the most salient indices of time-specific conditions. For example, a high level of life satisfaction on two days separated by a span of months or years does not even hint at periods of despair that may have occurred in the intervening time or at the ways in which the individual recovered from such depressed states.

We do not maintain that the collaborative interview or focused life history approach overcomes the dilemma. While we do gain some sense of both events and coping over time, we are seeing the process through the filtered eyes of someone who has had to come to terms with the past. We hear the stories, but recognize that they have been reformed by previous telling and reflexive interpretations. They are not "just the facts." Since we agree with phenomenological models of knowledge that argue that all so-called facts are interpreted and reformed in their apprehension (Merlieu-Ponty, 1962; Schutz, 1970; Kelly, 1986), it is necessary to listen and understand our data for what they are—our interpretations of the stories of individuals who are trying to make sense of the complex processes of their adult lives.

We will employ a number of indices that help place people in their social environments and give clues to their opportunities and orientations. Variables such as age index placement along the life course path. Gender and occupation suggest differences in expectations as well as opportunities. Resources are partly measured by income, family status, and education levels. However, none of these static measures does more than suggest

Life-Course Types:

1. *Straight Arrow* (40%).
   No major disruptions in the life course; expected transitions completed more or less "on time."

2. *Turning Point* (23%).
   One major trauma that required changes in life that impacted the remainder of the life course.

3. *Zigzag* (37%).
   Two or more disruptions that impact the context and resources of the life course with significant and lasting consequences.

Copying-Style Types:

1. *Balanced Investors* (40%).
   Two or more life domains are resources and loci of investment.
   Higher than average in life satisfaction, education, and occupation levels.
   Fifty-two percent (of the total of 48) was male (sample was 40% male).

2. *Family-Focused* (19%).
   Central support and investment in family.
   Above average in life satisfaction.
   Disproportionately preretirement in age, no college education, and industrial employment.
   Forty-four percent (of 23) was male.

3. *Work-Centered* (3%).
   Central investment and identities in work role.
   Three of four were women; three in professional/managerial occupations.

4. *Leisure-Centered* (3%).
   Central investment, identity, and community in leisure.
   Below average in satisfaction.
   Three of four were women; three in preretirement.

5. *Faithful Members* (4%).
   Central investment and community in voluntary organization.
   Average or above in satisfaction.
   Three of five were over 75; three were women.

6. *Self-Sufficient* (12%).
   Consistently self-reliant.
   No dominant external engagement.
   Varied in life satisfaction.
   Five of fifteen over 75; all but two were women.

7. *Accepting Adaptors* (12%).
   Passive: accept with little help and no direct action.
   Twelve of fifteen were women, and all but 2 were low in life satisfaction.

8. *Resistant Rebels* (2%).
   Blame the system, fight back from marginal position.
   Low in life satisfaction.
   Both male.

9. *Diffuse Dabblers* (3%).
   No consistent engagement or investment.
   Three of four had low education and occupation levels.

Figure 1–1. Life-Course and Coping-Style Typologies

something of the context in which the life journey has been made. They are useful, but not determinative. They give some idea of contextual parameters for the journey, but themselves tell us little about how life has been shaped within those boundaries. In no case can they even hint at ways in which individuals either hurled themselves against the limits in an existential thrust that might break accepted definitions of life or withdrew into behavioral modes defined by others.

One value in the sequential and multimethod approach adopted here is that we can compare results. In some cases, findings from the mailed questionnaire and its scales yield insight into questions raised in the intensive interviews. Comparing results of the telephone sample of 400 and the interview sample of 120 allows us to try to find answers to questions raised in the brief and highly structured telephone protocol. Yet, even with all the many kinds of data, we make no claims to comprehend the process of aging for Peoria adults. We have gained some insights and seem to have identified some patterns. We surely have added to that continual sociological enterprise of questioning some "common wisdom," what "everybody knows" about older people in America.

A Few Sensitizing Questions

In the next chapters, we will raise many questions and offer partial answers to many of them. However, before continuing with this presentation of that interpretive process, a few especially intriguing questions have already emerged from this introduction.

> What are the particular contributions of leisure to second-half life? If life satisfaction is distinguished more by the level of leisure activity than any other single factor (Kelly, Steinkamp, and Kelly, 1986b), what are the dimensions of that contribution?

> Is the traditional emphasis on "helpers" of older people slightly misplaced? Would it be more accurate to refer to "sharers" who have multidimensional relationships even with the "frail elderly?"

> Are the orientations and resources of women significantly different from those of men? What is indicated by the finding that women are much more likely than men to have adopted "psychological" rather than socially engaged patterns of coping?

> To what extent does social class determine not only the resources but also the world views of later-life adults? Are there taken-for-granted limits to life's possibilities that are a major factor in life-course patterns?

> What is "success"? Are some strategies of coping really more successful than others? And, if so, are they ones that can be adopted more

widely and encouraged by those in the helping professions, or are they not accessible to many in the real world of Peoria winters?

Preview

The remaining nine chapters of the book are divided into two main sections. The first employs the typologies to present and analyze the modes of coping with change through the life course. Most of the material is derived from the collaborative interviews and the interpretive processes developed. The second section approaches four problematic issues that are raised in the earlier analysis.

1. How is leisure a life course resource and for whom?
2. What are the salient factors in the development and maintenance of "social integration" and enduring relationships of communication and trust?
3. How do differences in opportunities and resources, the complex meanings of social stratification, present cumulative contexts of "making it" through life?
4. What are the main ingredients of success in life's second half?

References

George, Linda K. 1980. *Role Transitions in Later Life.* Monterey, CA: Brooks/Cole.

Glaser, Barney G. and Anselm Strauss. 1965. *The Discovery of Grounded Theory.* Chicago: Aldine.

Gordon, Chad, C. Gaitz, and J. Scott. 1976. "Leisure and Lives: Personal Expressivity across the Life Cycle." In *Handbook of Aging and the Social Sciences,* R. Binstock and E. Shanas, eds. New York: Van Nostrand-Reinhold.

Kelly, John R. 1983. *Leisure Identities and Interactions.* London and Boston: Allen and Unwin.

———. 1986. *Freedom to Be: A New Sociology of Leisure.* New York: Macmillan.

Kelly, John R., Marjorie Steinkamp, and Janice Kelly. 1986. "Later Life Leisure: How They Play in Peoria." *The Gerontologist* 26:531–537.

———. 1987. "Later Life Satisfaction: Does Leisure Contribute?" *Leisure Sciences* 10:1.

Merlieu-Ponty, Maurice. 1962. *Phenomenology of Perception.* London: Routledge and Kegan Paul.

Riley, Matilda W., ed. 1979. *Aging from Birth to Death: Interdisciplinary Perspectives.* Washington, DC: American Academy for the Advancement of Science.

Schutz, Alfred. 1970. *Reflections on the Problem of Relevance.* New Haven: Yale University Press.

Sennett, Richard, and Jonathan Cobb. 1972. *The Hidden Injuries of Class.* New York: Vintage Books.

Steinkamp, Marjorie W., and J.R. Kelly. 1986a. "Relationships among Motivational Orientations, Leisure Activity Level, and Life Satisfaction in Older Men and Women." *Journal of Psychology* 119:509–520.

————. 1986b. "Social Integration, Leisure Activity, and Life Satisfaction: Activity Theory Revisited." *Journal of Aging and Human Development* (in press).

Weber, Max. 1946. *From Max Weber: Essays in Sociology.* Translated and edited by H.H. Gerth and C.W. Mills. New York: Oxford University Press.

Part I
Styles of Coping
in Later Life

2
Balanced Investors

When the nine styles of coping with later-life change were developed, it was anticipated that focusing on resources and life investments related to roles would lead to a typology in which a single domain would characterize most adults. They would place greatest reliance on the relationships found in family, work, or leisure. They would locate their primary identity in one of the domains; give that domain priority in their allocation of time, energy, interest, and other resources; and in turn find there critical resources for coping with change. Further, we expected that the family would be the most common center of such meaning, investment, and help.

The likely exceptions might be those individuals of relatively high education levels with a breadth of cultural and developmental interests that would make them exceptional. They would be in professional or managerial kinds of work with considerable control over their work situations and clearly defined rewards for success. In their education, they would have had greatest opportunities to develop skills and interests that would lead to a fuller set of leisure investments as well as a more comprehensive hierarchy of hopes for the nurture and growth of their children. They would have interests and often competencies in the arts, have learned skills in "lifetime sports," and be discriminating about the quality as well as quantity of their children's education.

The expectations were not confirmed. The "family focus" was a significant and clearly defined life style. Two findings, however, required major alterations of the pre-analysis typology. One was the centrality of personal rather than resource-based styles for about a quarter of the sample. The second was that some balance among domains characterized far more of our collaborators than anticipated. Forty percent—the largest single category—was found to be "balanced investors." They had made salient resource investments in at least two of the three domains of family, work, and leisure and had received significant coping help in return. Further, the balance was frequently between family and leisure rather than work and other domains, especially if voluntary organizations such as the church were classified as leisure. As we will see, they were most likely to have high levels of satisfaction and some college education. They did not, however, all fit any stereotype of social elites with "everything going for them."

Mary's Multiple Investments Revisited

Remember Mary from the previous chapter. At age 62, she had been through two rocky marriages that ended in divorce, raised three children, cleaned houses and done laundry for others, and was over 50 when she began a real work career out of financial necessity. She was hardly the recipient of either a great start or of many breaks during the life course. Rather, her investment balance came out of a struggle to make it and a resilience that allowed her to overcome events that might have devastated others. Her zigzag life course had included "8 or 9" major surgeries, betrayal, physical abuse, and poverty. Without privilege or perquisites, she had created a life of balance and satisfaction. What are the components of her "balanced investment" style?

First, Mary finds significant self-definition in her office work, in her relationships with her "three wonderful children" and in their own growth into adulthood, and in her dance club and other leisure. Second, she receives strength and support from work friends, her sons and daughters, and her close dance club companion, Helen. Third, she has been consistent in her commitment to all three domains of life and acknowledges the importance of each. Fourth, she has given to, and gained from, each domain in an ongoing reciprocity. Fifth, she looks ahead to life with a continuity as other leisure investments will in time replace work. Sixth, she has changed and developed in each part of life with work and leisure providing important contexts for building resources and personal strength after the age of 50.

The balance is evident. So is the processual nature of the life course with its punctuating events, its closing and opening of doors, and the themes that have connected its periods. Mary has always been a responsible person in her relationships, even when there was every reason to abandon them quickly. She has never wavered from the centrality of providing a home for her children. Nor, whatever the circumstances, has she ever lost a sense of her ability to cope and do what must be done. No role or requirement has destroyed her sense of self-worth and fundamental competence. Even two husbands who put her down and attacked her integrity, one in mental illness and infidelity and the other in alcoholic abuse, did not destroy her strength.

Success stories are always reassuring. Mary, however, is not a "typical balanced investor." Her life has been too trauma-ridden and unconventional. There are two main styles of balance: conventional and high commitment. Further, there are differences based on where our collaborators were in their life journeys at the time of our study. Those who were in the "launching" period in which children had left or were in process of leaving home differed from the older persons who had retired from economic engagement.

Life-Course Types

Three life-course types were distinguished. For balanced investors, the sequence of life-course roles is important for the availability both of resources and opportunities. Family, work, and leisure contexts and orientations change as marriages develop or dissolve, children grow and inaugurate relative independence, work careers rise and ebb, and leisure abilities and expectations change. Mothers no longer have children at home to feed and clothe. Men and women are laid off or given greater responsibility at work. A player of team sports has to give up such strenuous engagement. Retirement brings a loss of work companions and a gain of blocks of time. That sequence varies in ways that impact every other dimension of life.

For the "straight arrow," life's transitions come predictably and on time. Role sequences are those that are expected with changes coming in the company of friends and neighbors making the same transitions. For "turning point" adults a single trauma, usually "off time," has required that every role be altered to cope with the changed circumstances. For the "zigzag" adult, several unexpected events have had impact on resources and contexts in ways that require major reorientation. Since balance calls for access to two or more major domains, it comes as no surprise that balanced investors are less likely to have experienced disruption. Half are SAs rather than the 35% of the remainder of the sample. Unlike Mary, they have most often had a regular sequence of work, family, and leisure opportunities. They have experienced fewer traumas and more continuity of life contexts. Therefore, we will examine balanced investment within each life-course type.

Straight Arrow Balanced Investors

One 40-year-old woman demonstrates ways in which progression through the life course shapes investment in life's domains. She is looking forward to playing more golf and travelling with her husband in a few years after her daughter and twin boys are launched. Her current involvement with youth-serving organizations will also diminish as will all the logistical requirements associated with their school and extracurricular involvements. On the other hand, the income from her job will be critical during the period of college costs. Her husband has advanced to the day shift at his plant and is less available for daytime driving and arranging. During this period of high demand, her leisure is mostly family-centered, augmented by church and occasional eating out. She hopes that abandoning golf and bowling is temporary and can be resumed when the parenting role becomes less demanding.

It is evident that adult roles are persistent even when their content changes. College-age children require financial more than logistical support. The key resource becomes money rather than time and energy. Marriages may shift more to companionship after launching. Work may rise in both economic and social salience. Personal leisure gives way to family expectations and contexts, but is not permanently abandoned. The life course shapes the orientations, demands, and schedules of central roles so that being a parent, worker, and player intersect every morning and evening in ways that shift through the years. Further, the constraints of each intersection seem to be accepted more than resented because they are expected and common to that segment of the journey. Therefore, we will separate the launching SAs from the retirement SAs in the following analysis.

Launching SAs: These individuals have begun or completed the process of getting their offspring into the big water of adult life, but are still engaged in their work roles. As a consequence, all the expectations associated with the care and nurture of resident children are waning. They anticipate or have fuller resources, both economic and temporal, than in any period since inaugurating their families. Most also expect to have several years of regular income before entering retirement.

Two styles of investment seemed to be common among our interviewees. One is characterized by a relatively high level of commitment to central life domains. Considerable drive and persistence are put into the roles of work, family, or leisure. These high commitment balanced investors are distinguished from conventional investors who more or less take the normal expectations and definitions of roles as they come. Conventional investors are less likely to persist in commitments when they encounter constraints and seem to have less keen experiences of satisfaction. When we contrast balanced investors with diffuse dabblers at the end of this chapter, we offer a continuum-of-commitment model in which the conventional investors are at the center of the bell-shaped curve with high-commitment investors at one end and dabblers at the other.

> Cal has found meaning that sets him apart from more conventional mid-life adults in sports. It would, however, be an error to suggest that he is a "sports nut" to the exclusion of work and family. At age 45, he has parlayed his education into a responsible management position and has been willing to relocate and change companies to achieve advancement. With two children still at home, he is

involved in parenting and believes that his marriage has been strengthened by more sharing of activity as the children have become less dependent. His central sports investment now is as a coach for youth hockey in a role that combines previous commitment with support for his sons. Further, he was willing to have his mother's stepfather live with his family for ten years. Despite family and work involvement, on the other hand, he played on no fewer than *four* softball teams last summer. When he ranks the leisure most important to him, the commitment is clear: youth hockey coaching and organization, attending sports events, and watching sports on television. His involvement has shifted gradually toward parental support and being a spectator. It would be interesting to find if his playing is dropped after another relocation that is ahead. While Cal would place work high on his value list and has taken his family roles seriously, his self-definition as a man has been tied to being an athlete and now a coach in ways that have changed through the life course but have remained central.

• • •

Eleanor, on the other hand, is more organizational in her orientation. She has retired as a school secretary at age 59. She and her husband have a relationship of easy communication and share their problems and concerns in regular conversation. Their adult children have been such a concern due to recent unemployment for the men in their families. Eleanor and her husband have given many kinds of aid and support daily during this difficult year. Launching has certainly not led to an end of responsiveness or responsibility. Nevertheless, Eleanor has a special set of engagements outside the home. She says she still first defines herself as a mother, but now devotes more time to volunteer work for the Salvation Army and her church. She enjoys reading, cooking, sewing, and the domestic crafts. She interacts almost daily with a close woman friend and frequently with extended family and other friends. She enjoys the freedom of launched children and no longer being employed. When asked about self worth, however, she referred to her volunteer work, to helping older persons through religious organizations, and to being of service. "There is enough to do out there if people will just get out and do it." Without any education beyond public school and with a world view of less than global horizons, Eleanor demonstrates persistent commitment as well as balance in her life investments.

Another male collaborator has had to reorient his sports involvement in his 50s because when you're older "You can't run, play basketball, and hunt the way you used to do." Now he reads more and is more active in his church as well as taking up the less strenuous sport of bowling. His adjustment has been facilitated by some friends having to make the same changes at about the same time in their lives.

Another pattern for those whose children are developing their independence but still live at home is to have life revolve more around their engagements. One father sees himself becoming more the "chauffeur" with less direct involvement in his children's activities. A university faculty member, he is quite engaged in his work and shares the parenting changes with his wife. Another compensation is the growing network of friendships initiated by his wife and often with the parents of their children's school, sports, and arts activity mates. For his own health, he runs regularly. His balance is illustrated by his complex schedule of work, individual activity, family support and interaction, doing "couple things" with friends, doing some consulting, and enhancing their residence. He believes he is interested in "too many things" despite having given up the outdoor activity associated with the Pacific Northwest resources they left behind to come to the midwest university. "Sometimes it all comes to a head," especially now that his wife is teaching part time. He is in a period of life that is encased in multiple demands based on his high expectations in all life domains.

Those who have high commitment styles in this high-demand period feel the pressure from outside and from within. Schedule synchronization and priority assessment are major agendas for their lives. The demands, however, are met in company with others who are dealing with these expected requirements at the same time and without major disrupting trauma.

There are also those whose levels of commitment are lower and who seem more to be responding to expectations rather than reaching out for meaningful involvement. These conventional investors were just as common even within the general category. A man with one of four children remaining at home has had the usual run of tasks and problems. He and his wife have had to place her mother in a nursing home. He lost a brother, his mother, and a close friend. His job is "O.K." despite some income reduction due to Caterpillar's economic difficulties. He has dropped sports due to an injury, walks and reads more, and teaches Sunday School in his church. He expresses some dissatisfaction about how "people expect you to be a certain way. You're never completely free." So "you compromise to a certain extent and feel a little guilty that you're playing a game." Nevertheless, he fulfills his roles and adapts to change. He is certainly "balanced" in his investments, but in a much more passive way than exhibited by Cal or others with similar interests and opportunities.

A 57-year-old woman who has launched three children is conventional in a somewhat different way. She has all the resources of economic comfort. She does not work outside the home and has substituted golf and bridge for weekday parenting. "Couple activity" is central, however. She and her husband engage in a full set of social activities such as entertaining and being entertained, dinner parties, and taking trips with friends. She is also a volunteer fundraiser for a community cultural organization, helps at a nursing home, and makes calls for her church. She is content with "how the kids turned out," enjoys people, communicates easily, and has accepted her role sequences without critical reflection. In her view, that's just the way life is intended to be. She has responded to expectations and opportunities in a conventional mode despite her high level of activity.

Harold is a preretirement straight arrow who seems to fall somewhere between the previous two in activity level, but is quite conventional. He is an easygoing and friendly person, 53 years old, who has come to terms with his priorities and investments. About ten years ago, he was not sure that his career advancement as an engineer quite matched his abilities and contributions. He applied to, and had interviews with, other companies. The negotiations proceeded far enough that he was required to evaluate his life and priorities. Eventually he decided that the relative security of the large corporation, although not perfect, provided the best basis for his entire life bundle. His three children were doing well enough in school and developmental activities that a change could be detrimental. Now he looks back at the decision with satisfaction. All three are professionals: one is a physician and two are engineers. His home and marriage are secure. At the time, his evaluation was, "Considering my family, where I was was not bad." Now he is more positive: "I have to admit that I feel that I have had it made since I got out of school." The factors are balanced: His marriage has "a lot of mutual respect." His children are turning out very well. He has done a life-course progression of organizational engagements— Scout leadership when his sons were younger, helping found a neighborhood organization, and his present involvement with the Shrine circus and children's activities. He gave up hunting and shooting, but now has a place on a lake where they can go on weekends. He likes to help others so tends to invest himself in an organization, "make a contribution, and then move on." Harold may be somewhere in the middle of that bell-shaped curve of commitment—engaged but without quite the enthusiasm or persistence that is exhibited by those of really high-commitment styles. All three domains of life are significant with family perhaps most fundamental. Yet, his sequence of activity and values seems more responsive than chosen and directed. Harold is conventional, partly by choice and partly as a consequence of his world view.

Retirement SAs: The conventionality of some launching straight arrows is reinforced in the cases of those of retirement years. There are fewer in the sample; the longer one lives the more often there are traumas. The regularity of the straight arrow life-course pattern seems to reinforce conventionality. The life journey proceeds apace, on time, and with expected sequences. There is less reason to question meanings as well as minimal need to cope with disruption.

> Muriel several times described her life as "serene." Her only daughter went to college and then married. Muriel was employed for 10 years, felt she had done enough, and retired to devote herself to her home and activities with family and friends. Her husband is a successful sales executive whose career has been a series of predictable advancements to a place of some prestige and security. The only disruption was her daughter's divorce after 10 years of marriage. She has now remarried and lives closer than before, about a half day's drive southwest. So, what has life become at age 66? Muriel and her husband visit their daughter as often as seems appropriate and are involved with grandchildren. They spend a lot of time with friends, some of whom are also neighbors, eating out and entertaining informally. They did their church office turn and now are less active. Muriel reads. She used to swim but gave it up when her beautician said she had to choose between her hairdo and the water. One close friend has moved to Florida and another died. Now she is going to have to cope with the next on-time circumstances: her husband's retirement and slowed mental alertness, other friends who will revise their residences southward in the winter, and her son-in-law's possible relocation. All this was explained directly and in a manner that suggested little in the way of questioning or reflection. Muriel seems to think that this is the way life is meant to be. Perhaps that is one basis for serenity.

Muriel may be more accepting and conventional than most, but she provides a useful "ideal type." Others in this category offer some variation on the theme. A 70-year-old widow helped her husband in his business until his retirement. She is more of an "organization person" than Muriel with consistent involvement in her church, a homeowner's association, a 50-Plus club, and a period of teaching ceramics. She summarized by saying, "My leisure is keeping busy." There had been an earlier period of depression that may be a spur to stay involved with other people in organized settings. She wants to avoid boredom and perhaps too much time alone with her thoughts. She and her husband only see their daughter and her family two or three times a year so fill their lives with friends.

Another retirement straight arrow had been a Caterpillar engineer. He enjoys retirement with its opportunities to take more time for activities and especially travel. He indicated that he really hadn't thought much about turning to others for help or advice. He and his wife take trips to "visit the kids" and entertain friends. He fishes some and enjoys the outdoors. Years ago, before moving, he had been on a small town Board of Education and sometimes misses that involvement. Now, however, more time and effort go into a "nice" home in a "good" neighborhood. He really hadn't given much thought to the kinds of questions about coping and investment that were raised in the interview, but had just taken life as it came along.

Men who are serious about their work and breadwinner roles are often complemented by wives who have major responsibility for home and family tasks. However, the men do share concern for their children and home. However commonplace it may seem to reiterate that they are "conventional," the adjective remains the best summary. These men have learned traditional role definitions and life course expectations in their parental families and socializing institutions. Little has hit their lives to require serious reorientation. So they have been "straight arrows" on both the smoothness of the life course and their definitions of what their lives have been about.

Turning Point Differences

Only 15% of the balanced investors had turning-point life courses. For both the launching and retirement subjects, some traumatic event or determinative condition made their investment patterns less conventional than most of the straight arrows.

Launching Turning Points: The nature of the disrupting trauma is significant in understanding the life-course investments of those in this category. A former beer truck driver had an accident, developed diabetes, and is unable to return to work. The onset of diabetic vision loss could lead to blindness, a possibility that this blue-collar man, who loved to hunt and fish with his buddies, has not really contemplated yet. In the past, he used to travel and go fishing with a brother, who died six years ago. He has also dropped bowling, Little League support, going to ball games with his son, playing pinochle with friends, and eating out. Now he watches more TV than he used to. Perhaps his most satisfying activity was building houses and garages with his brother. He still occasionally goes to Masons' meetings and hopes to duck hunt again. In general, this man seems to have found some meaning in work, family, and leisure without really making a high-level commitment to any one domain.

A much higher level of commitment was indicated by a 43-year-old gay man. He had been quite affected when his brother died of cancer while in college. His 20-year career at Caterpillar was interesting, but not so engrossing that he did not consider early retirement a possibility. Considerable investment had been made in completely redoing an older house with carefully wrought decor, but he and his companion hope to move south in a few years. His visits to the gay scene in Chicago are fewer now that he is in a stable relationship. The turning point in his life occurred over a decade ago when he sought psychiatric help after an intimate relationship ended. Now he accepts himself and has been able to build a life with a balance of work, financial security, home investment, leadership in an urban renewal program, reading, entertaining and being with friends, and care of his institutionalized mother. Most important, however, are his cohort of friends with whom his life style has been shared for up to twenty years.

Alice's divorce was the turning point in her life. Now she must work to pay the bills. A benefit, however, has been the transition to a belief in her own ability to make it through life rather than accept dependence on a man who wanted her in her place. Alice was a factory worker and also worked in a nursing home. At 49, she is totally responsible for herself and the son born just three months before the divorce. Her grown daughters, her mother, and a divorced sister provide emotional support and advice. Now that the plant where she worked is closed, Alice is making another adjustment: she collects unemployment benefits while she trains to be a nurse. At home she reads, quilts, and paints china. Outside the home, she replaced Girl Scouts with Boy Scouts, is involved in a church now that she is not ashamed of her divorce, and is an active member of the women's barbershop group, Sweet Adelines, in which she has followed her mother's interest. She is especially proud of her relationship with her step-daughter who "chose to be close" to her. She hopes for meaningful work as a nurse, is consistent in her devotion to the nurture of her son, and enjoys the singing group and church. All this was developed after her divorce to produce a varied life style that is satisfying in the knowledge that she did it herself.

Retirement Turning Points:

For Charlotte the real turning point among several difficult events was her second husband's death. He came home disabled from World War II and died when she was 35. Her first husband died in a car crash when she was 25, and after three miscarriages her one child born alive died after one day. Now 74, Charlotte copes with a mastectomy. The major change in orientation, however, came when she went back to school to begin a career in teaching after her second husband's death. With considerable support from her father and sisters, she got her Master's degree from Cornell and began a 25-year career teaching emotionally disturbed children. She retired at 61 when a boy lost control and injured her. Her life investments were her work, her home which she bought and improved, her church, and a number of community organizations. Leisure has been a source of stability in consistent engagements: reading, playing the piano and singing, a Music Club that meets monthly, a Woman's Club in which she has a number of friends, and the addition of Camera Club activity as she retired. She believes she has never been lonely because she has always enjoyed doing things for others and being with others. Most remarkable is the music group that began with high school conservatory friends and continues to meet monthly with the nine members still living. Charlotte returned to Peoria when her father's health began to fail. This return to her native environment also placed her in a social setting where the nuclear family was replaced by a network of friendship and sharing with other women.

Her story is similar in many ways to that of another professional woman. A never-married teacher and librarian found a social context for her life at the university. She had the financial burden of caring for her mother for years. Her present limited financial circumstances, however, are partly due to all the travelling she did during vacation periods while employed. Before retirement she took many summer tours and was quite involved in supporting the Peoria Symphony and the local theatre group as well as membership in the Woman's Club and the American Association of University Women. Now she listens to music on the radio, watches a lot of television, and is an AAUW officer. Her great loss is vision. She can no longer read or sew and is gradually dropping out of participation in evening social events. Now 75, the constriction of activity is due partly to the vision loss and partly to financial limitations. Nevertheless, her life pattern is one of consistent investment in work, friends, and women's organizations.

The once-common pattern of significant involvement in women's organizations by middle-class women is worthy of particular attention, partly because it may be becoming a thing of the past. "Career," even for these professional women, meant being a contributing member of organizations recognized as valuable to the community and that provided an opportunity for regular social interaction. The lives of many women were woven in and through such organizations that combined appropriate constructive projects with social engagement and recognition. They were valued and yielded identities of being worthy to their participants. The women were not just caretakers finding the meaning of their investment in the "success" of their children or workers receiving the symbolic valuation of an income. They were women working with other women to build and sustain a civilized community. For those women who had experienced a turning point, they often had special compensating functions.

Zigzag Balanced Investors

The zigzag life-course pattern is more common for balanced investors: 15 zigzags to 8 turning points. Perhaps the fundamental contrast, however, is with the balanced investors who have had more smooth and regular life courses. They have had the "luxury" of being more conventional because their changes have come predictably and on time or of being more committed because they have not had to cope with unexpected traumas. The wonder for some of the zigzags is that they have achieved balance in the midst of dealing with traumas. Exceptional yet exemplifying such resilience and investment commitment is a "launching" black woman:

Launching Zigzags:
Alma had ten children, two while in her 40s, one of whom died. She has been a leader and spokesperson for blacks in Peoria through the segregated 1940s and 1950s, the Civil Rights movement, and into the current period of "benign neglect." One daughter has coped for ten years with a progressive and debilitating nerve disease that drained family finances. Alma lost her mother and a brother and supported daughters through their divorces. She has the support of her husband, children, and friends, but gives the impression of tremendous personal drive and direction. Here is some of the evidence: She edits a newspaper for the black community in Peoria, ran for mayor, organized the first black Girl Scout troop and the first 4H group for black children, and has been on the boards of the NAACP, Urban League, League of Women Voters, and a number of local centers and projects. She was also PTA President at all three school levels and remains proud of her children and grandchildren. Three daughters have earned college degrees. Alma maintains a home in which extended family meet and mingle daily. Now 62, the breadth and depth of her commitments are awesome.

Alma is unusual, but the pattern of building and maintaining investments in multiple domains through a life journey dotted by disruption is not unique. One of the values of balance is that there are more often options in times of adversity; some doors remain open when others close. A second value is that personal and social identity are not all tied into one monodimensional bundle. When a spouse dies or deserts, a child disappoints, a job collapses, injury or age ends a sports career, close friends move, or health is shattered, there are other investments, other opportunities, and other identities. Here are two examples.

A 60-year-old man's wife died of cancer when he was 48, and his college-age daughter was killed a year later in an accident. He remarried after three years of trying to "do it all" as parent. His retail store did well and he expanded to a small chain operation. He had to stop playing tennis and bowling because of a bad back. He was involved in the Cancer Society, his synagogue, and the Chamber of Commerce. He worked hard in his business, provided a home, and supported his children through the periods of loss and readjustment. He believes that travel had a special function in providing opportunities for the family to get out of the environment associated with their losses. Now he feels "burned out" in a declining business climate and with the organizations in which he had invested. The next transition may be quite difficult because some of the old investments are fading in salience and satisfaction.

• • •

A woman in her mid-50s has just completed launching her children. She divorced when her children were ages seven to fourteen and remarried a year later. Her husband, with whom she shares little, was forced into early retirement when the Hiram Walker company closed. She has a secretarial position that she obtained after being unfairly fired a few years ago. A health problem has made sexual relations painful for her so she attempts to compensate in her marriage with super housekeeping. She helps care for her mother, worries about a daughter-in-law's cancer, and still mourns her father's death and a nephew's suicide. Her brother provided aid in tight financial periods, and she is close to her sister. Now that her children are grown, she is doing more things for herself—fishing, ceramics, sewing, bowling, and being with friends. She enjoys joking with other women in her office. There is nothing dramatic in this life pattern, but it all adds up to enough—work, leisure, children, and home. Life had indeed been a zigzag, but investments have kept things moving and together.

The traumas vary. Health is perhaps the most common. One woman had bypass surgery to help her cope with obesity, spinal surgery, and copes with arthritis. Her investment balance includes family, a business she began, church, gardening, jogging, and an exercise group. When asked who helped her cope with a series of personal and family setbacks, she mentions, in order, 1) the support of her husband, 2) her children, 3) a sister-in-law, 4) her mother, and 5) a friend.

Marriage problems are also common. One man, now 60, was divorced when he was 42 and became quite depressed. His second marriage has not turned out well. His wife is an unhappy person who offers more complaint than companionship. So, he gets away—to flying, boating, fishing, and his daughters from his wife's first marriage. He interacts regularly with other pilots and has a performance goal with his plane. His engineering work has been alternately satisfying and frustrating as management has changed. Cut off in his marriage investments, he has found satisfying identities in skill-based leisure and adopted daughters as well as the technical aspects of his work.

Like the straight arrows, zigzag investors may have high or low levels of commitment. The traumas in their lives have required them to be somewhat more inventive and less conventional. Nevertheless, at least two of the major contexts of life have provided associations, meanings, opportunities and identities that have given coherence and some direction to their life journeys.

Retirement Zigzags: The loss of the work context is another closed door for retired zigzag investors. A balanced pattern of investment focuses on family, home, friends and neighbors, and continuing involvement in organizations and activities. As persons move from "active retirement" years to frailty, there is a common social and geographical constriction of investments. Friends die or move away. It becomes more difficult to make it to sites outside the home, especially in winter. The financial, physical, or communication requirements of participation in some activities prove progressively difficult. In time, life becomes more and more centered on the home and immediate communities. For balanced investors, however, the active years of retirement often prove too busy, involved, and satisfying. They still have multiple avenues of engagement.

For one woman who took over her husband's business when he was incapacitated, retirement coincided with his death. She sold the business and invested the time in voluntary organizations, especially "Peoria Senior World." There she feels involved and worthwhile as she participates and makes items for the bazaar. She has also been able to reestablish close ties with her daughter who had been rejected by her husband. She babysits her grandchildren twice a week and helps a neighbor who has had a stroke. She is a "helper" whose orientations had for years been curtailed by her husband and who has been released by his death.

Another retired woman, a teacher, has had two major changes with which to cope. The first was the death of her alcoholic husband when she was 48. She had to move, cut expenses, and provide full support for her children's education. Later she experienced her daughter's divorce, some estrangement from her daughter-in-law, surgery for cancer when she was in her 40s, and a difficult change in her work environment. The second major change, however, was retirement which took her out of regular interaction with other teachers and out of the identity of an active teaching role. She referred to being "on the shelf" despite more engagement with reading and time for informal interaction with family and friends. But nothing has quite replaced the high school faculty lounge and the conversations over coffee and cigarettes. She is still in the process of making that transition by joining some study groups and becoming more involved in the association of retired teachers. One dilemma is that she doesn't want to be on a schedule, as she was for so long, yet misses the regularity of interaction. She is balanced, but her level of investments have so far been unable to rise to fill the reservoir of time created by retirement. One possibility is to return to some of the travel interests that she had developed when her children were first launched and laid aside when her time became more taken up with work and her daughter's post-divorce needs.

One limiting factor for zigzag adults is that of time. Coping with mutually reinforcing traumas of death or illness, financial loss, taking on multiple supporting roles, and coping with altered resources and circumstances has saturated the schedule. There just isn't much time remaining for exploration or new investments. As a consequence, the loss of work or family roles may require more reinvestment. Just carrying on established patterns, as most straight arrows do, is not enough. As with both the preceding cases, investment in organizations tends to pick up or redevelop interests and involvements from previous years. Those who have experienced multiple investments are usually able to reinvest when necessary.

Balanced Investors: Elements of Analysis

How do balanced investors differ from the sample in general? While the small sample requires considerable caution in interpretation, there are a few differences that are consistent with the material from the collaborative interviews. Table 2-1 summarizes the breakdown of background data.

Some of the comparisons are strong enough to warrant emphasis even with the small samples. Balanced investors are 70% more likely to have attended college than the sample as a whole, 50% as likely to be an unskilled or factory worker, over 50% more likely to have a high level of leisure activity, 30% more likely to have a high level of life satisfaction, and 50% less likely to have had a disrupted life course. Of course, the level of activity is an overlapping measure. The other differences, however, suggest that investors have greater personal, social, and economic resources. They are most often those who have gained skills and interests in higher education, have occupations with greater flexibility, stability, and rewards, and have

Table 2–1
Characteristics of Balanced Investors
(percent)

	Balanced Investors	Sample
Age		
40–54	29%	24%
55–64	27	25
65–74	35	32
75+	8	18
Gender		
Male	52	40
Female	48	60
Education level		
Less than high school graduate	12	28
High school graduate	21	25
Some college	27	23
College degree	17	12
Graduate study	23	5
Life-Course Type		
Straight Arrow	51	40
Turning Point	19	23
Zigzag	30	37
Occupation		
Unskilled	2	8
Factory	12	24
Sales or office	21	18
Self-employed	21	15
Professional or technical	40	26
Life Satisfaction		
Very low	4	9
Low	21	20
Medium	35	37
High	40	31
Level of Leisure Activity		
Low	2	8
Medium	50	62
High	48	31

N Balanced investors = 48
   Sample   = 120

avoided costly traumas. They have a stronger base from which to launch themselves into their investments. On the other hand, we should not overlook the fact that 40% did have turning point or zigzag disruptions, 33% had no college at all, and 14% were factory or unskilled labor. Further, they were only 30% more likely to have a high level of life satisfaction—a less significant difference than the resource base would suggest. One other difference will be examined separately; balanced investors were more often male.

Balance among the Domains

The resource differences are too important to pass by casually. They are not, however, separate and discrete. Rather, educational resources are complemented by financial resources which make possible travel, tickets to the concert series, and the purchase of books. Having a home large and gracious enough for entertaining complements having a wide set of friends made in professional and community organization contexts. Being free of chronic health problems leaves financial resources free for other uses and mobility and access to activities unimpaired. It is no wonder that balanced investors tend to have more resources and fewer impediments. The sets of resources are complementary.

In such the same way, the investments themselves complement each other. Education has been demonstrated to lead to both a breadth and depth of leisure interests and skills. Complementarity is also found in social relationships. Supporting children in their activities often leads to friendships with the parents of co-participants. Even for a 55-year-old ex-alcoholic divorced man, family and organizational ties reinforce each other. Five years ago he quit drinking, a year later had a heart attack and was then laid off from his unskilled job. He and his second wife live in a trailor, lost their car, and now live on a $5000 income, 20% of what they had before the heart attack. The church has become a social context in which he and his wife together can make friends and find support in their straitened circumstances. Now it is wife, friends, and church in a kind of package of involvement and interaction.

> For Emily, a 65-year-old retired teacher, the complementarity of the balance is supported by fuller resources. She and her husband are able to go to Florida for several months each winter. They are "best friends" and have become more conscious of the importance of what they share since his heart surgery. "When invited," they visit their adult children 200 miles away. Due to previous moves and their "winter break," they play less bridge with friends and are not as involved in volunteer work. She sings in a community chorus. They still participate in their church, enjoy plays and concerts, and play some golf. Their own companionship, which travels well, is the core around which the balance of activities is built. Leisure is seen as a context for making friends and being with others whom they enjoy. In retirement, activity investments have become a context for what they do together.
>
> Emily and her husband illustrate along with most other investors the "core plus balance" model of leisure (Kelly, 1983). According to this approach, most adults have a core of accessible leisure that is central to their life styles from early establishment on. The

core consists of informal interaction with others in the household as well as low-threshold activities such as watching television, reading, walking, shopping, and being with friends. The balance, however, tends to change through the life course as interests, resources, role relationships and expectations, and abilities change. The changes reflect the developmental preoccupations of their age in the domains of work, family, and leisure. For Emily, the balance had become tied to both continuing cultural interests and the organizational and environmental opportunities of their summer and winter retirement locales. The core, on the other hand, remained "familial" in a post-launching mode.

Age and the Construction of Life Styles

Age itself is an index of roles, opportunities, resources, and abilities rather than a direct factor in change. Variations in skill, health, interests, vigor, communication, and almost everything else are found for any age group or cohort. Nevertheless, as we age, we often must construct new patterns and styles of action and interaction or reconstruct older ones. For example, we found several widowed adults for whom a regular meal with friends at a restaurant is a significant combination of social engagement and nutrition. For some men, the preferred meal is breakfast. For both men and women, a downtown cafeteria provides the setting for meeting, eating, and talking. The establishment welcomes the older clientele, helps them with their trays, and gives them special friendly recognition.

Widowhood itself is such a significant change for most that it requires special attention. Among married balanced investors, the common pattern is that most social life is shared. Both middle- and working-class social circles in Peoria tend to be "couple based." The expectation is that married people will appear together in most settings except in those that are clearly oriented toward an activity with a gender bias or exclusion. As a consequence, widowhood calls for a radical revision of social styles. The reconstruction of life requires that new settings, engagements, and relationships replace the former couple-based ones. One of the benefits of balanced investment is that there are likely to be fuller, and more diverse sets of opportunities for such reconstruction.

Gender and Investment

Remember the cohort model of analysis for our collaborators. The women were born from 1900 to 1940 or so. They were students during the Depression, World War II, and in the immediate postwar years. For females in that time, the expectations and opportunities were rather different from those today. If women were employed, except during the warspurred mobilization-of-production period, the income was a supplement or a necessity and was earned in traditionally female occupations. Many kinds of leisure were considered unsuitable for the more delicate female constitution. A woman's "place" was in the home, no matter how necessary it was that she be employed elsewhere.

One consequence is that the range of activity for most women of these cohorts is more restricted than for men. Not only were women less often engaged in strenuous physical activity, but they were less likely to go anywhere alone, especially at night. Further, during childrearing periods, mothers were expected to give absolute priority to the care and nurture of their children. It was much more acceptable for fathers to have extra-familial investments. It is not surprising, then, that balanced investors are disproportionately men and women who have had professional careers outside the home. Women, on the other hand, more often have invested in "support" activity and those activities that include other family members. Balanced investment is not closed to women, but the domains of work and non-familial leisure have certainly been more open to men.

Voluntary Organizations and the Life Course

One dimension that is common for investors is participation in community organizations. Of course, the most common is the church. The second most frequent are those that provide supportive contexts for the development of children: Scouts, PTA, sports leagues, and others. For those with higher education and social status, there are the arts leagues and support groups. A surprising number of balanced investors have also been involved in community development organizations, social service, and church-based service. A few even participated in senior centers and programs.

Perhaps the most striking pattern is the extent to which such investments themselves have a life course. Only those who have older children still at home tend to remain active in the educational, activity, and sports clubs for their children. Activity-based clubs rise and fall in participation based on age-indexed likelihoods of ability. Consistent investments in operating the clubs, being an officer or managing programs, tend to diminish in the years just before and after retirement. When it comes to voluntary organizations, the balanced investor—especially the more conventional—tends to meet the expectations appropriate to age and social status.

The main exception is the religious organization, and even here older investors were less likely to be active in running the organization. Church often provided a context for investment and social integration with a degree of continuity. Even for those who had moved from one community to another, the church was a place to meet like-minded new friends.

Further, for turning points and zigzags with their disruptive traumas, the church was a source of support during the period of adjustment.

Much less common, even for these individuals of higher activity levels, were the activity-based clubs. Travel clubs, dance clubs, music groups, flying groups, and the like were quite important to a few of our collaborators. But they tended to be the exceptions. Rather, it might seem that our later-life adults were more often casual or life-course joiners than persons who found consistent meaning and integration in one or more community organizations. And balanced investors were more likely than any other major category to be in organizations at all.

Success in Coping

One factor evident in the relatively high life-satisfaction scores of balanced investors is that they were most likely to also be straight arrows. They had experienced less disruption and loss than even the family-focused. They not only had the highest levels of social engagement and resources, but also the greatest chance for continuity.

But that is only one side of the analysis. Balanced investors had taken action that tied them to other people as well as to contexts for learning and development and even for some engagement and excitement. They had higher levels of intensity and commitment as well as more relationships and ties. The remarkable story of Mary may not be typical, but it demonstrates how both continuity and novelty in multiple investments can provide a context for rebuilding a life from which most of the conventional supports and resources have been removed. Of course, there is also her sense of strength and direction that enabled her to seize and even create opportunities rather than be boxed in by the series of losses and betrayals. The same might be said of Alma, whose dedication to her family, her community, and to social justice seemed to plow right through the snowbanks of obstacles that might have buried some people.

The best model would appear to be a dialectical one. We cannot ascribe success only to resources: too many balanced investors had only modest means, education, or occupational opportunities. Nor can we argue that it is just a matter of personal characteristics: persistence, drive, and commitment. After all, many investors were more responsive to conventional roles than triumphant over obstacles. Rather, there were balanced investors whose commitment took them through barriers to successful coping. There were others for whom some combination of work, family, community, or leisure offered a context for coping in a more passive mode. What distinguishes the balanced investors of any commitment level or life style is that they give themselves to, and receive support from, at least two life domains. As we will see, that seemingly simple combination is not universal.

Diffuse Dabblers: A Contrast

There were only four diffuse dabblers in the sample. Diffuse dabblers are defined as those who shifted from one life domain and engagement to another without a high level of commitment to any. They had little continuity of attachment. One explanation for what they had done was that the activity had "filled time." They had little direction, tended to be bounced around by life events, and were unable even to articulate what they had missed. They are, in short, the other end of the commitment continuum (see figure 2–1) from the high commitment balanced investors.

The four dabblers were more different than one might expect. Two were male and two female. Three were under 60 years old. Two were zigzags, one was a straight arrow, and one was a turning point. One man had been married three times, laid off from several jobs, wandered rather than travelled, done some remodelling of houses, and tried several leisure pastimes. Another male dabbler is now retired and seems unable to find anything that does more than fill some time, although he does some gardening and has old cars around to work on. A 58-year-old woman is inundated with demands that she care for grandchildren, clean houses to make ends meet, and accept an unsupportive marriage.

All three of these dabblers are relatively poor. They have neither economic nor personal resources to expand life in a developmental mode. They have been disappointed in family ties. They tend just to "get through life a day at a time," not by seizing each day's offerings but in a dreary round. That is why the fourth dabbler does not quite fit the pattern:

> Virginia is wealthy. At 54, she is more than comfortable financially. Her work career has included teaching as well as management in real estate and travel firms. Her husband is supportive, and she has received help from her church and its minister. She plays golf, travels, takes walks, and works in the yard of their elegant home. So, how could she be a diffuse dabbler? First, her life fell apart when her son was angered by the sale of a family business in which he had been employed. He moved to California and remains estranged. Following this, Virginia went through periods of depression, cut herself off from friends, quit the country club, and generally found

Low _____ High

| Diffuse Dabblers | Conventional Investors | Committed Investors |

Figure 2–1. A Continuum of Commitment

any engagements an effort rather than a satisfaction. With its emotional and health consequences, her mother's stroke has also affected her. With all the opportunities that money can buy and a varied history of past work and leisure, she has not been able to attach firmly enough to anything to pull her through the family changes. Perhaps the point is that opportunities and resources are not enough. They do not inevitably lead to the kind of commitment that produces meaning.

In a simplistic way, all this sounds like a series of aphorisms: "You get out of life what you put into it." "Life is more than what you have; it is what you give." More sophisticated vocabularies would say that we are existential beings who must create meaning by our decisions and actions. As well, we are social beings who need trustful and caring relationships with others. Of course, the aphorisms could be true.

On the other hand, there are no guarantees. Balanced investors are more satisfied than diffuse dabblers but are not without their frustrations and disappointments. Further, the more conventional of the investors do not have a particularly high level of commitment or direction. Their satisfaction is so often expressed by some variation of "Things have come out all right" rather than by a recital of satisfying accomplishments. Nevertheless, balance seems to be better than its alternatives for most. Also, balance provides a model for comparison when we explore the other styles of coping with later-life changes.

References

Kelly, John R. 1983. *Leisure Identities and Interactions.* London: Allen & Unwin.

3
The Family-Focused

N at was introduced in chapter 1. His life journey seemed to unfold as a series of relationships and events that had no jarring disruption. Problems were dealt with in a context of what had become a four-generation extended family. His "household of children" is in reality a setting in which the generations have woven their lives together in ways that seem totally uncontrived. Nat and the others have other investments and other interests. However, Nat's life is clearly focused on the family. In a sense, all else is ambiance.

A family need not be restricted to nuclearity in associations or interests to be "family focused." For Nat, giving priority to the family is complemented by satisfying work, some special leisure interests such as his fishing trips to Alaska, and a sense that his life is of some value to others. Nevertheless, the core of life's meaning is in what he has given to, and received from, his wife, children, and grandchildren. There is no way of even beginning to explain what life is all about without this center of investment.

Dimensions of the Type

An "ideal type" is a construction of elements, all of which may not be found in any single case. However, Nat does exemplify most of the dimensions of the family-focused model. His values and fundamental way of viewing the world are family-centered. He invests his resources—time, finances, and energy—in the family's individual and collective enterprises. And he finds his primary resource for coping with change in the helping and sharing fabric of the family.

The three primary dimensions of the family-focused model are the following:

1. *Family-centered values and orientations:* This dimension is much more than a hierarchy of recognized values. Rather, the view of the world is from the family outward. Life is family-centered in the sense that the world is seen in terms of its intersections with the family. The self is defined within this solidarity. Decisions nearly always take the family into account. On the investment scale, the statement "My family comes first" only begins to tap the dimensions of this model. A dramatic example is the case of Jim who reconstructed his entire life formula around his family when he realized that his alcoholism was about to cause him to lose them. For those who have "launched" their children, being family-focused means that the meaning of the life course still has family as the central theme even though the nurturing demands have been relaxed.

2. *Family-oriented patterns of life investment:* Those who are in the childrearing phase of the life course may seem to have little choice about the allocation of resources. So much time is devoted to caretaking, money to child support, energy to the schedules and interests of children, and communication to negotiating the perils of parenting that little remains. However, for "second-half" adults whose children are either teens or living independently, allocation decisions may be more varied. Among our Peoria adults, the theme of continuing interest and involvement is common. Trips are frequently made to locations where children and grandchildren live. Entertaining means family first of all. The needs of children still take priority in time and financial decisions. In some cases, adult children have "bounced" due to divorce, unemployment, or some transition. They again live in the parental home, sometimes with their own families. In the midlife and later periods of summing up and making sense of life, marriage and children are the persistent dimension from which other domains take their meaning. "What has given you a sense of worth?" Over and over, we heard some version of this response: "The children have turned out O.K. despite some rough times." The journey to this point makes sense because family-directed investments have turned out all right.

3. *The family as primary resource:* It is more than a matter of a "return on investment." Those becoming old and frail may need to be cared for rather than able to provide support. For some, this shift is a gradual transition but for others it is trauma-induced. However, this fundamental pattern was found throughout later life. "Who provided emotional support during this change?" The most common answers for all types were some combination of husband or wife with teen or adult children. For advice and counsel, adults usually turn first to nuclear family, their own parents, brothers and sisters, and even "in-laws."

There are generational shifts associated with aging, but the connections within family circles remain paramount. Ellen, who has been a widow for 42 years, was employed for 20 years and quite active in community affairs. Nevertheless, it is clear that she derives most of her emotional support and counsel as well as significant sharing from her two sons who manage to include her in their own schedules and concerns.

Nuclearity and Separations

The "cozy cottage" image of the nuclear family does not characterize all who are family-focused. Some intact families have undergone periods of disruption such as alcoholism, unemployment, disabling illness, or emotional distress. The significance of family relationships and investments may have been poignantly dramatized by the death of a child. One mother was unable to describe the death of her daughter in a parachuting accident without breaking down. The event of many years before was still contemporary in its impacts on the weave of life's meaning. In fact, loss or disruption in nuclear solidarity seemed to accentuate the centrality of family for many in this category.

Threats to nuclearity come through the "off-time" death of a spouse or divorce. Being a single parent for 20 years due to the early death of a spouse or to divorce can create a pattern of family-centeredness that is a matter of necessity as well as choice. The straight arrow life-course pattern comprised only 40% of the family-focused. Two in the turning point pattern had lost a husband during childrearing so that the subsequent years were dominated by fulfilling all parental roles and requirements. Of the 23 family-focused, 17 had launched their children, two had lost adult children in accidents, and of two who were divorced, one was remarried. They are for the most part parents who have invested in their children and continue the pattern past launching.

Nevertheless, generalizations begin to disperse into uniqueness when the specifics of the journey are given attention. Each "story" has its own set of connections and self-interpretations.

Ellen is an 83-year-old widow living in a Lutheran Retirement Center. Her husband died when she was 41, leaving her the sole parent of two boys, ages 9 and 11. Since she had adequate financial resources, she devoted herself to "rolling up her sleeves" at home to fulfill her nurturing tasks until they left for college and independent family-building. Then she was employed in an office for 20 years before retiring. Ellen did not turn her life inward on the family to the neglect of the rest of the community. While the boys were in school, she participated in PTA, a music organization for youth, and church. She believes that then, as later, they "had fun together." However, the support and nurturing elements of her parenting role were preeminent.

When this role receded, she became engaged more fully in the cultural and organizational life of the community, especially music and volunteer work. At the same time, she enjoyed eating out and shopping with friends. In short, she took on some of the life style of conventional middle-class womanhood for her age cohort. The difference was that she had given extraordinary attention to being the sole parent of two boys. And in return, she received a high level of emotional support that she refers to as being "pampered." She evidently perceives considerable affective response to her efforts from her sons. Now that she is in an intermediate-care facility and limited by a colostomy that prevents her from being away from her bathroom for long, her sons continue the "pampering." The details do not seem unusual. They come by regularly and respond to her in ways that convince her of their affection and continued enjoyment of her company. As a result of what she perceives as this success with her primary life purpose, she is a relatively self-assured and socially confident person who has done well in the new environment of the Lutheran home. Both in the past and in the present, the center of her life is her sons and the reciprocal relationship of support and caring.

•••

Jim has quite a different story to tell. He and his wife have launched three children and now have grandchildren nearby. He finds a sense of accomplishment in that and in having completed payments on the modest house they have lived in for 29 years. They have also bought 80 acres of "farm" land in Wisconsin and think about moving to Texas and doing more fishing someday. Now at age 51, Jim would appear to be a typical construction/factory worker who has achieved the blue-collar American dream of owning his own home, preparing his children for a better future, and anticipating a retirement with grandparenting and fishing in a warmer climate. Such a picture would be quite misleading. First, Jim has been only intermittently employed for three years as the Caterpillar Company economy of Peoria has fallen on lean times. He has secured just enough employment to keep his benefits coming and tried to "keep halfway busy with work on the house." Jim and his wife go out to eat less often. He skipped his annual hunting trip to Wyoming with a cadre of friends, the activity that he "enjoys the most." Jim tries not to become anxious over this condition that poses some threat to his future hopes and plans. As a sometime construction worker, it may seem only an intensification of usual conditions in that industry.

However, this uncertainty is viewed as minor compared with the major turning point in Jim's life. Jim had been an alcoholic with a rather flamboyant leisure style. He had been a professional—if not too successful—motorcycle racer who travelled the Central states weekend circuit with a buddy. He also flew old two-place airplanes as a hobby. Also, he engaged in regular in-season weekend hunting in Illinois and Wisconsin. His life style was pointed outward at "masculine" and excitement-oriented activity with like-minded other men. Amid all this he drank, a lot. Finally, his wife forced him to choose between his family and liquor. With the help of professional counseling and Alcoholics Anonymous, he quit drinking and remains sober. His life style change has been dramatic. Although he still has a road bike, he no longer races. Nor does he fly or go hunting often. Now his family members come first. His pride centers in their mutual support. When he wanted to stop drinking, it was his daughter who made the appointments for group therapy. It is now his wife to whom he would turn first for emotional support and counsel. He didn't drop his old buddies; "they dropped me when I stopped drinking." He still enjoys hunting—occasionally. But now leisure consists more of eating out with his wife, being with the kids and grandkids, and seeing some new friends. He knows now what he wants as the center of his life. Without being especially analytical or engaging in self-recrimination, Jim has constructed a new life style around his new set of values.

Other examples of variation from the neat and traditional family–life cycle course are found among the 23 family-focused individuals. There is a widower who has been lost since his wife died, a widow who is quite lonely after losing her husband of 53 years, a divorced mother who had to rebuild after her husband ran off, another ex-alcoholic who gambled away the income that might have provided a little comfort, and others whose primary focus on the family have come through hardship and change. Cherished children have died tragically. Sons have had mental breakdowns, lost their jobs, or undergone their own divorces. Placing the family first is no guarantee of tranquility or of secure later years. Nevertheless, it is one viable life style: for many it is the only one ever considered.

Diffuseness and Large Families

In this day of one or two children, carefully planned and produced in a compact time period, we may forget that large families were seen as quite natural for many in age cohorts now in their 60s, 70s, and 80s. Nat, of course, with his children and grandchildren nearby is a prime example of investment in quantity as well as quality. The pattern is one in which children and then grandchildren are a continually changing developmental context for the life course. Giving, sharing, nurturing, supporting, and enjoying are all elements of the relationships. This context is what life is all about, a generally unexamined definition of life.

However, the large and extended family has its negative aspects as well. Anna is the mother of 12 children. All have left home, but now she takes care of grandchildren in the daytime. In fact, she has been caring for children for 41 years—since she was seventeen. Her zigzag life course has included economic deprivation, health problems for herself and her husband, and a difficult divorce for a son. She has a very low score on the life satisfaction index that is illustrated and compounded by her life story. She is family-focused and invested, but in a ceaseless and unremitting way that has considerable impact on the investment returns. Nurturing and launching 12 children yielded no respite since she now seems to be expected to care for grandchildren to permit their parents to be employed. However, she is employed as well. In the evening she leaves for the office sector where she is a night janitor. While the children were still at home, she worked in a school cafeteria until her blood pressure forced retirement. Now she is just tired all the time.

Anna has had gall bladder surgery, a bad back, and hypertension. Her time is filled with responsibilities that admit little in the way of relief or intermissions. Her husband, a part-time Baptist minister and blue-collar worker, appears to be peripheral to her support system. Her children helped some when she had surgery, but evidently expect from her more than they give. Church is her only outlet, but even there she finds people friendly but not a source of relevant support. With children and grandchildren filling her apartment on a Saturday afternoon, she seems very much alone. When asked about sources of self-worth and meaning, she didn't seem to grasp the concept. She is simply overwhelmed by family and worn down by the added requirement of off-time employment, which would be exhausting even for someone younger and in better health. She may need relief—some time and space of her own—that might be called "leisure." But now she is just *tired* with little sense of any way out or perspective on what it all means.

• • •

Eva also has a life deeply intertwined with extended family, but in a more positive mode. She also experiences family obligations and worries, but casts the entire set of responsibilities and relationships in a positive definition. Two sons were launched and one has now returned to join in the family contracting business. Eva and her husband take care of grandchildren, sometimes for a week or so at a time. However, this conventional level of nurturing was not enough for them. They also have taken over ten foster children for months at a time. They have found profound meaning in investing them- selves in the lives of others. The question of self-worth is no problem for Eva. She immediately begins to speak of children who had been abused and rejected. Her regret is that they didn't have a larger home so they could have done more.

She is religious to the extent that she believes that God is her first source of support and help. However, this is in the context of mutuality and sharing with her husband, her sons, other kin, and a woman friend in the neighborhood as well as competent case workers. The family's varied leisure is family-oriented in which camping, skating, bowling, or travel are primarily vehicles for informal interaction. She belongs to a group that provides regular religious services at a retirement home and has also welcomed foreign students into the home. The main problem now is the state of the economy in which construction is so slowed that the business shared by her husband and son is in trouble. What was intended to be an extended opportunity and resource as her husband would prepare for retirement from Caterpillar has become problematic. They have too much involved to quit and not enough income to provide a viable base for two families. As bookkeeper for the busi- ness, she sees the numbers regularly and cannot help but worry.

Nevertheless, Eva is a person who has given extensively to others and received a full sense of meaning and accomplishment in return. She has no extensive cultural interests. Like so many of the family-focused, she has only a high school education. Her life style is one of nurturing that never gives real consideration to the possible separateness of one life from others. She is deeply con- nected in an immediate social matrix that is multi-generational and that creates as well as accepts "family." The primary meaning of work, leisure, and community—as of life in general—is family- focused.

The differences between Anna and Eva are more than attitudinal. The number of children is, of course, critical. With 12 children and overlapping sequences of caring for grandchildren, Anna's situation has been over- whelming and unrelenting. Eva has been able to make choices, to choose investments rather than be buried by obligations. There is a clear difference between having modest but dependable financial resources and living always on the margins of security. There is a difference between being able to invest in foster children and having to come home from night work to an apartment filled with grandchildren. There is a difference between choosing companionship as leisure and not even recognizing the possibility of choice in the use of time. Both women are family-focused, but with marked differences.

Most of the family-focused fall somewhere between the two extremes in satisfaction and orientation. For example, a 67-year-old woman has six children and 19 grandchildren. Although the family is central to her life interests, she also enjoys working part time, travelling with her husband, and a new interest in computers. Her enthusiasm is expressed when she exclaimed, "With a family like mine, how could I not want to spend my days doing things for them?"

A preretirement-age woman with nine children has yet to experience the completion of launching. Two children are still at home. She was disturbed by the divorce of one son, especially troubling for a Catholic family. Her husband had undergone very serious brain surgery and then retired early. His being "there" all the time requires some adjustment. However, they hope to buy a sailboat, spend more time with family and friends, and enjoy the timetable freedom. She sees her life as not particularly stressful, perhaps due to the immediacy and dependability of the family system. She likes to travel, eat out, and entertain friends. She is conventional in values and aims. Her summing up is spoken with satisfaction: "I have raised nine children and they have all turned out well. My life has been mostly wrapped up with my family." Her values and her opportunities have been coincident rather than conflicting. As a consequence, her life course has been one of development in which anticipations were met with actualization. Even major disruptions can be encompassed in this family-centered security. Satisfaction does not mean a life without problems, but one in which what was most important worked out.

Multigenerationality and Meaning

For many later-life adults with a major familial investment, grandchildren are highly significant. They offer continuity in nurturing, a sense of contribution, and an opportunity to renew familiar roles without the "everydayness" of parenting. Of the 23 family-focused cases, over half gave considerable emphasis to the importance of sharing the lives of their grandchildren. Nat was unique in the geographical clustering of his extended family, but not in the satisfaction and meaning found there.

Grandchildren are usually perceived as a joy. Nat's ongoing involvement with his children's children is more than a responsibility or a satisfaction; it is as much a part of life's environment as air and water. Eva has enjoyed the return of a grandchild to the immediate family context although she worries about the business being a viable means of support. Other adults with children who are now rearing another family generation plan trips to visit those who are distant, keep up on the telephone, and even remain in a home large enough to accommodate visits. Those whose grandchildren are nearby become babysitting resources, share in family outings such as picnics, and spend time on Saturdays shopping for gifts. Anna's grandparental burden seems to be the exception although it might be much more common in neighborhoods of extreme poverty and truncated economic opportunity.

> Earl had a history of family connection. His wife's mother was the hub of the family network. "Wherever Mom was, the family could always get together." Since her death, the adult children have rotated care for Earl's father-in-law whose three-month stays alter their freedom for engagement outside the home. The two grandchildren, now 14 and 17 years old, are more than an extension of the family line. Shopping often includes planned or spontaneous purchase of things they might like. The grandparents attend school and sports events from baseball to the marching band. In early retirement, Earl and his wife have the opportunity to "do everything together." Their most valued leisure involves their interaction with the extended family. Many social activities are related to their grandchildren's engagements rather than being with peers of their own age. In fact, even the fishing trips that were enjoyed a number of years ago have been curtailed as the combination of family obligations and investments has come to dominate the allocation of time and other resources.

One couple plans their trips to Missouri to coincide with the special events of their grandchildren and seems always ready to adjust their busy community schedules to a Peoria visit. Several grandparents talked about building their social schedules around their grandchildren's school and other events for several years. Jim had even become a scorekeeper for his granddaughter's softball team. Others use the telephone to keep up between shared events. "What do you hear from the kids?" is a common question at the dinner table of these homes.

For a woman in her mid-60s, launching was defined as a period of loss even though the children remained in Peoria. Later the birth of grandchildren enabled her to regain some of that nurturing dimension. In fact, she now reflects on the times she might have been more accepting and less rigid with her own children. When her father came to live with them for six years, her freedom was severely limited. As the primary caretaker, she seemed to have lost almost all free time, even though her husband tried to help. In retrospect, however, she believes that the responsibility pulled the family together as even the grandchildren helped out. She also has a neighbor-friend who came over so she could go shopping and who has remained a close confidant through many years. Her leisure activity is primarily couple-oriented—going out to eat and taking short car trips. As for Earl and his wife, their grandchildren's activities—especially school sports—were an important part of their schedule during their period of participation. Now their modest means allow for slightly longer trips and a little more freedom in their timetables. The importance of family-centered periods, however, is symbolized by the pictures of individuals, groups, and events that cover the living room walls.

Grandparenting is for many family-focused persons an anticipated and "normal" sequence in the life course that seems to offer many of the joys of cross-generational sharing without quite the commitment of resources. The powerful impacts of divorce often include a disruption in the relationships with grandchildren that emphasizes their importance. The loss may be felt very sharply. Further, a grandchild's illness or accident may be devastating emotionally for the grandparents. The emotional investment in grandchildren is a major theme of many later lives. Again, this investment is symbolized by shopping habits, the scheduling of vacations and trips, and a general synchronization of timetables to facilitate interaction.

Of course, several of the adults in this study had experienced the "sandwich" effect in which they were caretakers for older kin in failing health while still having considerable responsibility for their children. In some cases, the sandwich had a third layer—concern for grandchildren as well. When the layers of relationship overlap to create an overload of demand, the family focus that had been a matter of choice and taken-for-granted life style may develop dimensions of duty and obligation that alter resource allocation, possibilities for choice, and definitions of the meanings of relationships.

Resource Allocation

References have already been made to a number of ways in which resources are allocated by family-focused adults. When resources—time, space, energy, emotional attachment and expression, interest or orientation, and financial decisions—are defined inclusively, then allocation demonstrates the pervasive nature of the central life investment. The common indices of resource investment follow.

1. *Household Timetables:* Both daily schedules and seasonal calendars are developed to respond to the engagements of others in the extended family and to opportunities for interaction. Vacations as well as weekends are scheduled around such opportunities. Numerous telephone

calls may be required to sort out the conflicts and coordination. The "where" as well as "when" of vacations are negotiated with the extended family. The priority that such negotiation is given is demonstrated by the common pattern that it precede other arrangements in temporal order of decision-making.

2. *Space:* Couples may remain in housing too spacious for their own needs so that there is "a place for the kids and grandkids to come." Just as period in the family life cycle may have been a major factor in earlier housing choices, so location and access to grandchildren may be given precedence in retirement location choices. Our sample from a "sending" rather than "receiving" retirement location included only those who had chosen to stay in Peoria—often for family and financial reasons.

3. *Energy:* At any age, there are limits to the amount of energy available for demanding activity. Therefore, the priorities given to the use of energy may be a good clue to relative values. For older adults, that supply of energy may seem to be even more limited than it was earlier in life. One grandfather rationed his energy by allowing only one grandchild to visit at one time. More often, other engagements are postponed or eliminated to give priority, for example, to a dinner for the children or a trip to a granddaughter's first recital.

4. *Affect:* There may not be the same limitations on emotional attachment and expression, but allocation policies exist nonetheless. Family-focused adults expect to give and receive most of their affection and emotional demonstrations from family members. Although the nature and even spontaneity of affective interaction tends to change through the life course, in American culture the family is expected to provide such outlets and responses.

5. *Interest:* In interviews with family-focused adults, the liveliness of the presentation tended to be markedly higher when family was being discussed. Attention is a major factor in what we see, how we sort out the stimuli of our environments, and the symbols to which we respond. For these men and women, the family was clearly the center of attention. Not only enthusiasm but the ways in which family attachments recurred throughout the discussion of almost every aspect of life indicated that there is a giving of attention as well as an attention-commanding presence in family relationships.

6. *Decisions:* "What did you do then?" was a question we asked repeatedly in the interviews. In relation to most changes, the family-focused responded with some variation of a family-oriented decision. Caretaking, support, sharing, an adjustment of schedule or other relationships, or some other response to family need or opportunity characterized the transitions of the family-focused. Decisions are made with the

family first among those who are considered salient. "How will it affect spouse, children, or other kin?" is the first and sometimes only question to be answered.

The Family as First Companions

Of course, those in one's household are the most available for almost any activity. They are often the "companions of convenience" as well as of choice. And those who are most accessible are not always those who offer the most satisfying companionship. Further, there are times and places when we are responding to the expectations of others and even attempting to avoid their disappointment.

Simply having companions available is no small matter, especially for those in life's final years when many family and close friends may be dead or incapacitated. A less-than-fascinating companion may be better than none at all. Many people simply do not like to go out to eat, travel, attend concerts, or walk in the park alone. For older women safety may be a concern. Even without a high level of communication, having someone to go or be with may be quite significant.

However, the quality of the companionship is also an issue. Earl has restricted his own range of leisure, especially fishing in Minnesota, to meet the caretaking needs of his father-in-law since his mother-in-law's death. Retired for two years, Earl and his wife "do everything together." Relationships with his wife, daughter, grandchildren, in-laws, and friends come first. He has largely dropped fishing and golf despite the fact that fishing in the Northern lakes was an environment in which he felt most free to be himself. At age 62, Earl has constructed a life pattern around familial companionship.

Two family-focused women, also in their 60s, also place high value on such companionship. One enjoys her children, but also appreciates the time now available to be with her husband and to become closer to him. About ten years ago, she had a heart attack that curtailed her work after 37 years in a factory. She has also had to cope with diabetes and regular insulin injections. However, her life is filled with family and friends. Support from her husband in adapting to the diabetes is complemented by her two grown children and especially a daughter-in-law with whom she feels comfortable. She likes being with her four grandchildren, a close friend and "fishing buddy" who lives across the street, and other friends with whom they sometimes eat out. She has become reinterested in the church in the last few years, perhaps partly as a replacement for the parents' groups she joined when the children were home. However, it is clearly the companionship with her husband that is the central theme of her activity. She says, "I enjoy being with all of them, but my husband, I really enjoy being with him." Fishing, playing cards, eating out, or just sitting in the back yard are all activity environments for this companionship. Her life seems simple and lacks a breadth of interests which reflects the fact that she never finished high school. Overall, she is quite satisfied with her later years because she has never been without the opportunity for sharing her life with those who matter most to her.

The second woman, now 63, has a graduate education and worked part-time as a librarian after her two children left for college. Her husband is required to travel for several days at a time in his sales position. This meant that she had the primary responsibility for childrearing during the week. Now she is occasionally able to go along on his trips. A somewhat tense person, she valued the support and "problem solving" that took place on weekends. Her children live at such a distance that they exchange visits only two or three times a year. Also, she has been quite troubled by a son's divorce. She has friends. However, it is the quality of the relationship with her husband that is critical. Weekends are the focus of her personal and social agenda. During the week she reads, gardens, and does a little volunteer work. It is the weekend set of social events and interactions shared with her husband that is most important. Her high level of satisfaction is based on an adjustment to that schedule restriction and on the quality of the weekend and travelling time they have together.

Does this suggest that the quality of communication and interaction among some long-married couples is high or instead, do some women settle for routine companionship? While there may be some of both, among our family-focused older men and women the accounts of regular sharing and support in times of trauma suggest that there are lines of strength in many such relationships. Carlos has moved from Central America and endured a series of immigration problems that has intensified his conviction that having the family together is the most important thing. Another man travels with his wife to the South every winter, but never goes to the same place twice. Every trip "is like a new adventure." They rely on each other for companionship in a new social environment each year. They do nothing else that is unusual in their retirement years except for the support and care they give their granddaughter who has lost a leg to cancer. When in Peoria, they take her for chemotherapy treatments and try to help her parents who are both employed. His interview does not suggest any remarkable level of communication, but rather a quiet kind of support and sharing that enables them to deal with traumatic events as well as with changes they have sought.

There are several recurrent themes in the accounts of companionship. One is the evident significance of the marriage relationship in later years for the family-focused. For those in intact marriages, "couple" activities and relationships are paramount. A second theme is adaptation to launching by continuing to share their children's lives when possible. A third is the importance of such activities as travel and eating out as contexts for the relationship. The different environments give them something to share, a change that may enhance communication with something specific to anticipate, plan, experience, and recollect.

Nurturing as a Life Style

One persistent theme of family-focused life styles is nurturing. Eva with her children and foster children probably exemplifies this dimension most fully. However, the theme is a common one. It is partly an investment in children. The central preoccupation during childrearing periods of the life course is to provide a context for the growth and development of children. To some extent, this is carried out in economic functions of providing a home, food, clothing, education, and other care. However, the greater investment is of the self in orienting adult lives toward children. Nurturing is more than a requirement or even an aim; it is the pervasive way of life that colors every decision or resource allocation.

The clearest indication of the centrality of this orientation is found in responses to questions about what had contributed most to our subject's sense of worth and value. Over and over the responses pointed to parental involvement in the life course of their own children. They had given of themselves in manifold ways. The satisfaction, so important to most of the Family-focused, was that "the kids have turned out well." Emotional bonding with their children is made up of so many elements—so many shared experiences, so much care and worry, and so much unquestioned giving— that particular events are difficult to highlight. Especially for many of the women, whether or not they shared childrearing with a present and involved husband, the affective sharing and caring as well as the hopes and plans of nurture were what life is all about.

Who Are the Family-Focused?

What are the common elements in the 23 case studies? What kinds of backgrounds seem to be most likely to produce adults with this style of life and meaning?

We do not have complete life histories on our subjects. The intent of the study was to examine social factors in coping with later-life changes, not to reconstruct a full birth-onward story. However, as outlined in chapter 1, there are some differences in background and resources among those demonstrating the nine types of coping styles. Table 3–1 provides a display of such variables for the family-focused.

Table 3–1
Characteristics of the Family-focused
(percent)

	Family-focused	Sample
Age		
40–54	30%	24%
55–64	30	25
65–74	22	32
75+	17	18
Sex		
Male	43	40
Female	57	60
Education level		
Less than high school graduate	35	28
High school graduate	43	25
Some college	9	23
College degree	9	12
Graduate study	4	5
Life-Course Type		
Straight Arrow	39	40
Turning Point	30	23
Zigzag	30	37
Occupation		
Unskilled	9	8
Factory	43	24
Sales or office	24	18
Self-employed	14	15
Professional or technical	10	26
Life Satisfaction		
Very low	9	9
Low	13	20
Medium	35	37
High	43	31
Level of Leisure Activity		
Low	9	8
Medium	65	62
High	26	31

N   Family-Focused =   23
    Sample   = 120

The family-focused differ from the full sample of those engaged in the collaborative interviews in the following ways:

They have lower education levels; only 22% attended college at all.

They are more likely than the sample as a whole to have been skilled workers or foremen in factory settings.

They are slightly more often in the pre-retirement age categories.

They more often have high subjective well-being scores and are less likely to be at the low level.

Is there any way to sum up these tendencies? A profile would suggest a man or woman who has made the family his or her central life investment in a real choice but with narrower options than some with more educational background or a more stimulating work setting. However, the differences are not dramatic. Leisure activity levels follow the overall distribution closely. As will be discussed in chapter 7, leisure engagement was found to be the most significant correlate to life satisfaction. Therefore, the family-focused, who are more likely than others in the sample to have a high level of subjective well-being, must find such satisfaction in their family investment.

To sort out the elements in such satisfaction, we need to turn back to the content of the interviews. In general, the family-focused seem to believe that their lives have been both personally satisfying and worthwhile. One factor seems to be the immediacy of the significant others. Life is concentrated on those who are, at least for many years, right there. Lifelong contact provides ongoing feedback. This concentration on immediate relationships also accounts for the lower measures of satisfaction among those who have been left alone.

A second dimension of this relative satisfaction with life may be found in the value system represented. For the most part, the family-focused are rather conventional. They place high value not only on their children, but on having avoided real trouble. They tend to be quite troubled at the divorce of a son or daughter and seldom speak of conditions that might have made the divorce an improvement in life conditions. They tend to live in modest detached homes and are proud of ownership. They are often religious and receive reinforcement in their family investment patterns from their church associates. Their leisure has been centered around the family including participation in support activities when their children were in school. A common outside engagement for men has been fishing, often in company with nuclear or extended family. Surprisingly, after launching their children, the family-focused do not tend to widen the range of their leisure. More time for travel is frequently directed toward the locales of grandchildren. In most cases, husband-wife companionship is reported to be a major meaning of travel.

The family-focused, then, seem to be almost a stereotype of the conventional family with limited educational and occupational resources. They have turned their lives toward the most available source of meaning and satisfaction. They have supported their families and usually experienced some positive return on that investment. Again, we have to turn to the singular profiles to recall the variety that belies too great an emphasis on the general pattern. We should not forget the ex-alcoholics, the tragedies of the loss of spouse or a child, the women who were single parents most of their adult lives, the immigrant who has struggled to keep his family together in a new land, and the grandmother who has never known relief from childcare.

To complete our analysis, we will re-examine some of the particular aspects of the lives of the family-focused: leisure, work, resources for coping, gender differences, and the family as investment context.

Leisure for the Family-Focused

The clearest indication that the leisure of the family-focused is oriented to family companionship and interaction is in responses to the question, "What two kinds of leisure would you least want to give up?" This question has been found in previous research to elicit a relative value or centrality set of responses. Of the 23 family-focused types, 18 mentioned informal family interaction or "visiting family and friends" among those most salient kinds of leisure. Of the five exceptions, one was never married, one widowed, and one divorced.

The stories are just as clear. Vacations tend to be family trips. The homes of those children who have moved away and have produced grandchildren become primary destinations. Those who are nearby are sometimes companions on trips, especially for fishing or camping. However, they are more frequently the companions for entertaining, eating out, picnics, attending various events, and just being together. Grandchildren are taken to special places. When older, their events attract the attendance of grandparents. Most important, leisure plans generally take into account the schedules and commitments of extended family so that special events, child care, and other synchronized occurrences can be coordinated.

As already suggested, companionship is a recurrent theme in the stories. While the likelihood that couples would engage in considerable leisure together was no surprise, the emphasis placed on companionship was. Literature on the meager and strained communication in such working-class marriages documents a lack of positive affect and sharing (Rubin, 1976). On the contrary, several of those in this study spoke quite strongly of the high value they place on what they do with their spouses. Launching and retirement provide a freedom to eat out, travel, and do other things together.

Leisure is generally defined by the family-focused as a context for the expression and development of primary relationships. This seems to be the case for those who have undergone dramatic change in their lives as well as those like Nat for whom the life course has unfolded pretty much as hoped:

Ray is 53 years old, has only a few years of grade school education, and is black. Two of his six children still live at home in a very simple apartment. He lost his retirement benefits when the plant he had worked at closed. He now drives 60 miles to another job. Previous plant closings had caused him to move his family and to lose homes they had begun to buy. Ray is functionally illiterate, has no financial security, and is dependent on transferable job skills. Five years ago, Ray realized that he had spent the money for his children's Christmas presents on alcohol. With the support of his wife, he stopped drinking. Now he looks back with great regret at the costs of his alcoholism that will continue to be paid by his family. However, he has a positive attitude toward his life. "I feel better and I am doing the right thing!" His wife, a deeply religious woman, provides not only companionship and support, but also a remarkable demonstration of building his sense of worth. She tells how now the whole family comes to Ray for help and advice. His leisure is simple. Television is important because it costs so little. Otherwise, he directs his attention fully to his wife who has become his "best friend and companion" and to the children. He knows he cannot make up for all that has been wasted, but that doesn't stop him from trying. They can't afford to do many things they would like, but they are able to share what is possible. Since he quit drinking, Ray had to reconstruct his leisure life to replace his former companions. He has done so by becoming fully family-focused.

• • •

Ethel had a different kind of trauma. Four years ago her husband ran off with the wife of a close friend. Now 55, with her three children launched, a high school graduate who was never employed, Ethel rebuilt her life with leisure and the companionship of family and friends. She sees her children and parents almost every day. She has close friends whom she sees at least once a week. She watches lots of television, especially during the week. When her husband deserted her, she felt "dumped on" and quite devastated. Her husband had never been around much to share in childrearing, but had nonetheless provided a measure of security. Urged by her teen and young adult children, she joined a church-sponsored divorce seminar, played golf, joined some clubs, and traveled. She is selective about her leisure activities and has added hospital volunteer work which helps her feel useful. Her parents, children, and friends assured her that she was a worthwhile person who could make a success of a different life style. Before the divorce, her life was almost totally home-based and centered around her children. After a year of emotional anguish and self-pity, she began anew. After a time, her ex-husband died, leaving her a share in his business that has provided financial security. Later her son divorced, an event that forced her to relive her own pain. Ethel's is not an unmitigated success story. She is moderately happy, but knows that life has not worked out as she had anticipated. She does not like this feeling of dependency, partly related to her lack of education and skills. But she has rebuilt a life that combines regular interaction with extended family and engagement with others through organized activity.

For both Ray and Ethel, leisure is an important element of rebuilding their lives. Ray now devotes his time and energy to his wife and children. His limited resources are employed to try to compensate for all the waste of his drinking years. Ethel is quite dependent on her adult children, parents, and friends. However, she has branched out from her former home-bound life style to regular association with others in clubs, volunteer work, travel, and sports. With the help of those close to her, she is beginning to believe that she is a person of worth whose life is far from over.

Leisure, then, is a context of interaction and communication for the family-focused. It is "relational" in valuing such interaction rather than seeing it primarily as an obligation. However, leisure is also a resource, especially for those whose lives have been disrupted by trauma or loss. Leisure complements rather than conflicts with the central life investment in family.

Work as Instrumental

Work is not the center of life or identity for those who are family-focused. How much of this is a positive value placed on the family and how much a lack of engrossing opportunity in employment is difficult to determine. Only 24% were professional, technical, or self-employed. Over 40% worked in factories. Perhaps it is not fair to analyze in detail interviews that concentrated more on family and leisure than work. However, we did ask specifically about work changes, roles, and meanings.

The typical family-focused man has not had a work career with an escalating progression through positions in which productivity in one period leads to advancement in the next. Further, the economic climate for heavy industry in Peoria had turned from security and growth to recession. The women in this group tend to take on employment in a very instrumental mode. They add to family income, become breadwinners in the absence of a male provider, or view their employment as supplemental to their husband's primary earnings.

Whether the lack of opportunity for an identity-providing work career or investment in the family came first, the family-focused in the sample seldom referred to work as providing their basic sense of worth, their most significant relationships, or their hope for the future. For almost all, the meaning of work was found in what it made possible for the family. Employment paid for the house, made nurturing and education possible for their children, and supported their life style. Income was defined primarily as a resource rather than as a symbol of status or success. This seemed the case for all of those whose cases have been examined in detail.

Resources for Coping

Two kinds of resources are most frequently mentioned. The first is financial. Recalling that most of the family-focused had wage-earning jobs without either security or an income that would permit much investment, the probability that other family members might need financial assistance is high. A life-cycle approach would suggest a later-life switch in the direction of support. Through education, launching, and early establishment periods, parents might be expected to help their children. Parents in their 50s, with earnings peaked and children who are coping with the demands of establishing a childrearing household, may help with downpayments, special gifts for grandchildren, and backup income in times of unemployment or illness. Then, in retirement years, this help reverses direction as the adult children supplement their parents' reduced income.

The Peoria family-focused included only five persons over 70. Of those, none were receiving one-way financial aid from their children. Three were comfortable to the extent that they retained the pattern of special gifts to grandchildren as well as financial independence. Two widows who were poor shared such burdens with children. One lived in a retirement complex with her daughter. The other, of course, is the 58-year-old woman who works at night and cares for grandchildren in her home during the day so her daughters can work. She receives some payment for this service, but the implication is that such recompense is irregular and small.

For the family-focused, the main issue is emotional support. Such support includes a number of dimensions. The most important is expressed by the now-common phrase, "He (or she) is there for me." It builds confidence to know that when needed, a son, daughter, spouse, parent, or sibling will be available and "on your side." One form or another of this theme predominates in the interviews. We asked about changes related to work, family, marriage, residence, and health. Then in relation to particular events we asked "Who helped?" "What was the nature of that help?" Then, to examine particular dimensions, we probed with questions about advice-giving and counsel, community resources, and support in self-definitions of worth. For this typology, the responses were consistent and clear.

Usually there is a primary support-giver. Most often for those in intact marriages, it is the spouse. Some version of "When things are difficult, we always talk it over" was the recurrent theme. For those who had been widowed or divorced, the source of support was most often teen or adult children. For example, when life-threatening surgery was impending, a daughter who is a nurse came from California. When a husband ran off, it was children who were there and who insisted that the devastated mother get on with rebuilding her life. When a widow needed counsel, she turned to her adult daughter who lived 200 miles away. Each story has its unique elements, but the general theme is clear. Family members are "there for each other." It is a priority, a taken-for-granted premise of living, and an expectation.

In fact, it is the exceptions that tend to capture our attention. Nat, Eva, and others with multigenerational family environments may have some difficulty specifying which kin have helped the most. "It depends on the kind of advice I need," responded one widow. It is the ex-alcoholics with their stories of support from wives and children, the poor whose children still need help, the mother upset by a son's divorce who nevertheless tried to give support, the self-assured widow with ample financial means who just wants her sons' companionship, and the retired couple who have tried to help when a granddaughter was undergoing chemotherapy that are a little different in the general picture of continuing reciprocity and responsiveness. Support means companionship for many of these later-life adults. Remember the retirement-age woman who seemed so spontaneous about being with her husband, whether at home, shopping, going fishing, or eating out with another couple. Emotional support for them is nothing special; it is the atmosphere of living.

What Is "Success?"

The question of success in coping with later life needs to be addressed. Success is only partly indexed by subjective well-being and scales of life satisfaction. Rather, successful coping with change and trauma must be understood within the value systems of the subjects. For the family-focused, that value system revolves around intimate relationships, relationships with children and "how they have come out," and being able to maintain a context of interaction and emotional support.

Again, the exceptions come to mind first. Anna, the widow with all the children and grandchildren, has a desperate struggle just to get by. Women who had invested themselves in home and family are profoundly upset when a husband took off with someone else. For them, family now means the children who rally around to help. There are the frail widows and widowers in ill health who depend on family for almost all forms of support. But they are the exceptions in this study.

For the most part, the relatively high levels of life satisfaction scores among the family-focused are consistent with their stories. They have invested themselves in a domain of life that is accessible and responsive. There may have been disappointments along the way. For two women, the tragic death of a child can never be forgotten. Nevertheless, on the whole, the family investment is worthwhile. Most with this central orientation seldom consider alternatives. Maybe they are "conventional," but it has seemed to work for most of them. Investment and support yield a proximate and satisfying meaning for their lives.

Gender Differences

Some might expect that in a society with clear sex-role expectation differences, family-focus would be found primarily among women. Especially for the cohorts now in their 50s, 60s, and 70s, bourgeois value systems support the idea of women as nurturers and caretakers whose realm of meaning is primarily familial. Further, the extrafamilial opportunities for women were quite limited in the 1930s and post-World War II decades. The exception was wartime when women were pressed into economic production roles.

In this study, there is no clear gender distribution difference in general orientation. Men are as likely as women to define their lives in terms of family and finding the meaning of their economic roles in the home and resources they had been able to provide. The socialization of men as well as women in conventional working-class homes is often toward the family as primary. This might be intensified by ethnic value-systems, especially from Latin and southern European Catholic cultures.

There are differences, however, in the content of the roles. Among these families, the investment still has a primary "provider" role defined for men and "caretaker" for women. The chief exceptions are the cases of women who become single parents in their earlier childrearing years. They were required to combine the roles. This gender distinction should not be taken to the point of dichotomy. Companionship and nurture are important to the fathers in this coping type. And many of the mothers had at least supplemented household income. In fact, considering the conventional values and the historical era of socialization, the mixing of role orientations might seem more pronounced than expected. One reason is necessity. Most of these families were never more than days, weeks, or months from exhausting their financial resources.

Family Focus as a Theme

One danger posed by the format of this analysis is that the typologies are presented as more distinct and different from each other than the data warrant. As already presented in the previous chapter on the balanced investors, family contexts and priorities are significant for most later-life adults in that most common life style.

Family-focus is a significant dimension in the life of many of those classified in other coping types. Family is in some degree a central value and investment as well as resource for those adults who cope with change in balanced, self-sufficient, or accepting modes. In a few cases, the lack of a familial context is the prime factor in the adoption of another style of coping with later-life change. This is especially true for women who have been denied a central family investment opportunity. As we will see in later chapters, patterns of acceptance or self-sufficiency in some cases are precipitated by a closing off of other options.

Family focus is a major investment style as well as a common theme among contemporary later-life adults. Its roots in the culture are reinforced by conventional, religious, and ethnic values. Further, for most adults the family is "there." It is the most persistent and proximate realm for investment and source of meaning and support. To an extent, some lives may even be defined by a lack of this context and resource as much as by the styles of coping that are adopted.

References

Rubin, Lillian B. 1976. *Worlds of Pain.* New York: Basic Books.

4
The Work-Centered, Leisure-Invested, and Faithful Members

The two major resource-based coping types—balanced investors and the family-focused—together account for almost 60% of the sample. The three types introduced in this chapter are less than 11%—only 13 of the 120 of the intensive interview collaborators. They are the "specialists" who have not achieved a balance among life domains or invested themselves primarily in home and family.

As indicated in chapter 1, the small size of these categories might be surprising. Where are all the "Protestant ethic" types, those who may not be "workaholics" but find their primary identity in work? Are all the allegedly self-preoccupied and leisure-focused individuals identified by the mass media under 40 or living in California rather than Peoria? And what about the "nation of joiners" who have been a part of folk sociology since the days of the French visitor DeTocqueville?

One answer is simply that we didn't find them. If they exist in large numbers in American society, either they are somewhere else or our small sample didn't happen to pick them up. Our study suggests that those who have been so sure that work, leisure, or membership in voluntary organizations is central to many adults have concentrated their research on those dimensions and measured those concepts to the exclusion of other dimensions. Our strategy of employing change and coping as the windows through which to view investments and resources is not biased toward any domain unless it is toward those that are most consistent through the life course.

If, then, those who have constructed their lives around their work, leisure, or membership in voluntary organizations are exceptional, why are they different? What factors in their lives can be identified as crucial in their unusual life patterns?

One principle of scientific explanation is "parsimony," that is, using no more elements or details of explanation than are necessary. The most parsimonious accounting for this small number who have focused their lives around a single domain other than home and family would be based on an analysis of their access to resources. Do all or most of them tend to be cut off from the domains that might have permitted a more balanced or family-focused investment pattern? If there is a clear pattern of deprivation or blockage, then we need not delve into more complex sociological or psychological accounts.

Opportunity Theory and Work or Leisure Investment

The work-centered not only invest themselves in their work role, but identify themselves primarily in terms of their work. For example, they are teachers or engineers first and parents or church members second. The leisure-invested also define themselves primarily through one or more leisure commitments, and allocate most of their discretionary resources toward that domain. If opportunity explanations can be sustained, then it should be possible to locate a "push" away from other possible domains as well as some "pull" toward the work or leisure investment.

> Don illustrates both the attraction of creative work and the depri-
> vation associated with minimal family engagement. Before his
> retirement two years ago, he had a career in product development,
> first with a small company and then in a large hierarchical firm. He
> is very proud of the 24 patents registered in his name by his
> employers and what he sees as his contribution to the technologies
> of contemporary living. In fact, the greatest change with which he
> had to cope was when he moved from the informality of the small
> company to the bureaucracy of a large corporation. There his
> functions were valued in an impersonal mode and his relationships
> determined by the status hierarchy. He no longer had lunch with
> the company president or even his immediate supervisor. The
> security in health and retirement benefits, now important after
> bypass surgery, more than compensate for the loss and necessary
> adjustments in work style. His wife, on the other hand, seems
> secondary if not peripheral to his life. She had concentrated on
> parenting until launching was completed, had some sort of break-
> down, and coped by seeing a psychiatrist, taking valium, and
> getting a job. Don's preference for a role-segregated marriage style
> as well as his personality offered her little in the way of support or
> reorientation toward the marriage dyad. The push away from
> home seems more a product of role definition than a fundamental
> deficit in Don's wife. Now even a shared interest in the grandchil-
> dren who occasionally visit has not radically altered the retirement
> separateness of their lives.

How, then, has this work-centered man who lacks close relationships at home or among old work associates coped with retirement? In short, he has found a new "job." He is doing research and preparing to write a book on family genealogy. His attitude toward this "leisure" is very task and product-oriented. In a sense, he is still working—now in an area that offers the opportunity for a product that he can be proud of and, more than in the large corporation, control over the conditions of his work. In the interview, Don brought every question around to his work: his 24 patents, the work environment transition, and the book he was going to write. His deprivation may have been partly of his own construction when he failed to share significantly with his wife. However, his life course was his own, not a dual-track. He and his wife are not a "social couple," he says. He enjoys his genealogy club as he enjoyed work associations, especially in contexts where he received recognition. His leisure, like his work, is characterized by performance: "doing it well" and receiving recognition for his accomplishments.

With such a small number of work or leisure-centered adults in the sample, numbers have little meaning. The push and pull of opportunity, however, are also found in the coping styles of others. One woman with a zigzag life course invested herself in a leisure engagement after having other doors shut in her face. As with Don's retirement shift, her leisure and work became blurred during a significant transition. She was divorced three years ago after 21 years of marriage to an alcoholic who abused her physically and emotionally. She is remarried, but her life remains more oriented outside the home. Her main avocation, home decorating, has now become her vocation. After being laid off from the job she secured during her divorce transition, she has tried to develop her leisure preoccupation into an occupation. Decorating is more than an activity; it helped her "keep her sanity" when she "drove (herself) to keep busy." When couple associations were reduced, she was helped some during this period by Parents Without Partners. One couple—her "best friend" and her husband—provided significant counsel and support.

Deprivation may provide a push toward a single focus on work or leisure, but there is also the possibility of choosing a life orientation with a central attachment to work or leisure. An individual is so attracted to that life domain that it comes to dominate patterns of investment. Not only is the self defined by that role, but other engagements are clearly secondary in salience.

The farm, in her husband's family for over 100 years, is the center of a 50-year-old woman's activity. When their sons left home for school and other lines of work, more and more of the farm work load was placed on her. The constant preoccupation is this year's crop and keeping the farm afloat financially. She has given up substitute teaching, adjusted to the death of her son due to cystic fibrosis, and reduced her leisure to farm-related organizations, church, and exchanging evenings at home with friends. Her choice to be work-centered is constrained by economic necessity, but is also a choice based on significance of the investment.

• • •

Perhaps more typical is the 69-year-old retired teacher who never married. After caring for her parents, both of whom had strokes, she continued to teach young "culturally deprived" children in one of the older sections of Peoria. Her complaints about the adding of educational technologies to replace classroom interaction were voiced through the teacher's organization in which she was active. Health problems including a mastectomy have lowered her energy level. A reflective person, she has learned to adjust to change. The real center of her life, however, was her work and her workplace associations. Organizations such as one for retired teachers, her church, and some volunteering keep her in touch with others and in a helping and nurturing mode of association. In a retirement center, she reads and talks with friends on the phone. Her work gave her life shape and meaning, especially since her family roles were filled by parental care and then emptied by their deaths.

• • •

A business woman, age 63, also never married. Her sister, although not a companion, has moved in and out of her home several times. She had to find a new job a few years ago when her firm closed, not an easy task "when you're a woman in her 50s." But she secured a better position and wonders why she didn't change years before. Her closest friends are not at work, but in a businesswomen's service club. Her work is her identity, and her social group is other women in business. Her home is "a place to live." A cottage on a Midwest lake is less attractive now that it always involves her sister.

There are also a few in the sample who have been so drawn to some aspect of their leisure that it has become life's central domain.

Cliff has moved from the East Coast where he loved to visit the ocean beaches, not for swimming, but for the ambiance. Now 54, he he gave up sales work, took a job with "Cat", and now is responding to a layoff by starting his own business. Why has he stayed in Peoria? Because his children are doing well there, but even more because he found a special place to live. He has an isolated home in the middle of a forested area where wildlife is all around. His outside associations are with nature conservation groups. His leisure is otherwise at home: walking, reading, listening to music. He does Audubon bird counts, cares for his three dogs, two cats, and one snake. He mostly engages himself in the natural rather than social environment. His family is important; his work instrumental. His leisure is more an environmental immersion than "activity." Nevertheless, it is the central immersion of his life, the focus around which fundamental decisions revolve.

•••

For Cliff, the environment was primarily a pull that became an organizing principle for his life. For Amy, a woman of about the same age, leisure was instead something to cling to when almost everything else seemed to fall apart. Despite her ex-husband's series of affairs, her son has blamed her for the divorce. She has not seen him for two years. Her father died at about the same time as the divorce. Her blood pressure is high. Amy has not been employed for over 20 years. Her finances are limited to her half of the value of the house and $260 per month from her ex-husband. Nevertheless, she is determined not to "let the bastard get me down." She fills her life with friends with whom she attends plays and concerts and goes out for dinner. Leisure settings are her major locale for social interaction. Such engagement is also a help in re-establishing an identity as someone other than "Mrs. _____ ."
Just getting up in the morning has been hard enough. Caring for a mother with cancer has added to the emotional and financial strain, but also required her to get out of the house. The push of the divorce and son's attitude is balanced by the pull of her love for the arts and the companionship of her friends. Her leisure-investment is somewhere in the middle of an opportunity-deprivation continuum of explanation. Amy is still so much in the process of recovery and rebuilding that her adaptive success remains uncertain.

•••

For Clara, however, the zigzag course of life has not led to much success. She gave birth to her first child at age 17. Her daughter eloped at the same age. Her son moved back at age 23 with no means of support. Her husband's life of drinking complicated by diabetes changed when he was 60 and was told he was about to kill himself. Clara's best friend died recently. Now 67, she cannot read or sew due to deteriorated vision so she watches TV and talks on the phone. She used to go to bingo with two friends, the one who died two months ago and one who is now too "feeble." With all this, Clara has developed a mental condition in which she has a low energy level and is reluctant to leave the house. Medication and a short hospitalization led to enough of a recovery so she is no longer blocked by fear from answering the door, crossing bridges, entering elevators, or other phobias. Little has happened to her to counter a poor self-image reinforced by her early divorce and a doctor's advice that she should quit work because it could be a cause of her second husband's drinking. There is little attractive power in Clara's modest leisure; she just doesn't have much else.

What appears to be almost totally missing in this study is a series of stories of people who love their work to the exclusion of almost all else or are so engrossed in a leisure commitment that they cannot be understood apart from that role (Stebbins, 1979). We need to remember that some who are now more balanced or family-centered were much more tied to their work or leisure when they were younger. Work and leisure commitment may be less one-dimensional than we supposed when formulating the study. Further, those with a consuming work or leisure focus may be concentrated among those under the age of 40.

In our few cases, focus on work or leisure seems to be as much or more a matter of push than pull. The never-married are denied the familial investment. Others turn to work or leisure in situations of limited family response or integration. If family is "where, when you go, they have to take you in," then for a few leisure and work may be where you go when they don't. It is true that most have a series of jobs, not a career. It is also true that some get little return on family investment. Ironically, most of those who find greatest meaning and fulfillment in their work seem to be balanced rather than single-minded.

Social Integration and Community Organizations

Five collaborators were found to be "faithful members" whose life context and meaning were centered on some community organization. They are like the family-focused in several ways: they tend to be conventional in their values and orientations. More important, they have made community organizations the central theme of their investments. Again, there may be deprivation for some. For most, however, a particular organization or set of organizations has come to provide the relationships around which they weave the schedules and commitments of their lives. And for the most common such organization, the church, there is also a set of ideas and beliefs that provide meaning as well.

The zigzag life course of this 72-year-old woman unfolded in an interview marked by her forthright and clear expression of both the events and how she understands them. Bridget was the youngest of ten children. Her coal miner father lost his disability pension for blindness because he refused to give up ownership of their little home. Bridget left school after eighth grade to help support her mother. From her childhood she doesn't remember having a single toy; "We were lucky to have food on the table." Other disrupting events included moving to Peoria, the "big city," when she was married, having urban renewal threaten to take their home, a son who disappeared for four years after his divorce and then telephoned threatening suicide, and a lingering illness of her husband prior to his death four years ago. Now she is in a retirement home.

How has Bridget put together a life of meaning and worth through all this? And how has she overcome the sense of inferiority caused by the economic and educational deprivation of her childhood? Her grandchildren help by coming regularly to take her out into the community. The central focus of her life, however, is religion. She is a lifelong Catholic whose traditional faith was given an intensity of personal meaning and commitment by her participation in a movement called "Kirseal." In this program, laity gather for a weekend of lectures by clergy and other laity on the significance of their faith in coping with problems and decisions. Those who emerge from the intense weekend with a new commitment then form a community of support for each other and for newer members who "make Kirseal." The experience was important for Bridget's coming to love herself and gives her a sense of fulfillment. She and her husband also became involved in interdenominational evangelistic religious groups. In fact, Bridget lists the Christian Broadcasting Network on cable television as her chief media interest. She is concerned about "witnessing" about her faith to others and special masses with emphasis on healing and "speaking in tongues" as well as more conventional church guilds and services. For her it is all there: community, mission, meaning, and a sense of worth and contribution. Her life is so enmeshed in the various segments of her religious commitment that nothing is interpreted apart from that set of relationships.

A retired Salvation Army officer also demonstrates this centrality that can come with such a religious commitment. Even though at age 84 she now misses the regular responsibilities and involvement that shaped her life for so long, she still makes the Bible study and weekly meetings with other retired Army personnel her personal community. For her, as for Bridget, there is the attraction of satisfaction and reliable community as well as a sense of purpose.

There is also, however, a deprivation element to some faithful member-ship. Four of the five are widowed and the other separated. The differences in patterns seem to be more ones of timing:

> Two, Bridget and the Salvation Army retiree, have the continuity of religious commitments that have been central for many years.

> Two have become deeply engaged in groups for senior citizens in their retirement years, but in styles that are carried over from previous engagements.

> One, a former barge loader, is a lay evangelist in his black church organization. It is all that seems left for him now that he cannot work, is desperately poor, lives in a shack, and has been left by his wife and estranged from his daughter. Now he "saves souls" and suffers in order to reach heaven when he dies.

Two faithful members, then, have long-term religious commitments. One simply has nothing else left. The other two have taken engagement styles into the organizations that are best designed for their period of the life course. This involvement in organizations for older persons is rare enough in our sample to merit special attention.

A 79-year-old widower is continuing a helping mode of participation. He has a history of being a "helper," an advisor, and a caretaker. The oldest of 11 children, he was relied on for help more than being one who received assistance. Now he is active in several seniors' organizations: he is a member of the county council on aging, treasurer, and the one who sends birthday cards to members of one club, active in a church "golden age" group, and so on. He travels a little, plays cards, and eats out. But mostly he is a proactive helper of his peers through his organizational attachments.

A woman of 82 is a more passive participant. She copes with health problems through her "faith in God" and the community provided by church and community seniors programs. She joined the groups after her husband died so that she would have companions for travel, going to plays and shows, and filling her time. With less than a high school education, she depends on others' initiative for transportation and companionship. She joined "on time" and participates as programs are offered.

Transitions, Commitments, and Deprivation

It is risky to attempt to derive patterns from only a few cases. Nevertheless, a few "working hypotheses" are suggested:

1. Religious organizations to which a central commitment is given provide more than a social context. They are a community of meaning in which the relationships and rationales for action are mutually reinforcing.

2. There is a measure of deprivation in some long-term religious commitment and community. Economic and educational deprivation, however, are not the entire basis of such central affiliation. Rather, a sense of mission and being of service to others are endemic to such communities. Such religion is more than Marx's narcotic for the dispossessed.

3. For the organizations designed for older persons, there seems to be a pattern of "on time" transition. Either as a faithful member or a proactive helper, the recruit may find the peer group an alternative to familial community lost in widowhood or other familial limitations. Note that for professionals, retirement-based organizations may be work-related rather than open to the general population. Then some work-based identity is retained along with the advantage of shared histories.

The two themes that dominate these cases are the need for an organizing principle for life and for community. Often a concentration on work, leisure, or a voluntary organization for these life dimensions is related to lack of opportunity: those who have not married turn to work, those who have lost community find it in organizations, and those without a career orientation find meaning in a religious commitment. The old pattern of nurturing work for never-married women leads to professional associations and attachments. The meaningful community of the church seems a compensation for a lack of diversity and balance for some whose life circumstances have been limited. Through crisis and change, single attachments and significant organizations offer both a sense of worth and a context of community. Neither may offer the versatility of balanced investment or the immediacy of the family. Yet, a single focus on work or leisure or finding community in active membership are a response to opportunity as well as to doors closed to other contexts of action and affiliation.

References

Stebbins, Robert. 1979. *Amateurs: On the Margins between Work and Leisure.* Beverly Hills, CA: Sage.

5
The Self-Sufficient

The first question in developing the typology of coping styles was that of resources. In which life domains are central investments made and crucial support offered? Family, work, and even leisure in some hierarchy or combination were critical domains for most of the 120 collaborators. But for almost 30% of the sample, no realm of resources was dominant. Rather, their styles of coping with change were based more on their own attitudes than on social roles.

As we will see, the analysis does not switch to psychological modes at this point. First, we did not employ any instruments that purport to assess psychological states or personality types. Second, the three non-resource types are still social in that they define an attitude or position in relation to the world. "Self-sufficients" turn away from external to internal resources for coping. "Accepting adaptors" take a passive stance toward the impingement of external events while "resistant rebels" attempt to fight back. Third, self-sufficients have social histories with common themes. We will not argue that events have created self-sufficients, but that certain kinds of events seem to be common to most who develop this style of dealing with later-life change.

What is self-sufficiency? First, it is a self-definition of independence. Self-sufficients define themselves primarily as individuals rather than as members of any group including the family. Second, it is a position of self-reliance in coping with external events. Third, it is a strategy of self-management that does not rely on others, individuals or institutions, for either help or direction. Unlike the family-focused or faithful members, there is no community or group ideology that shapes response patterns. The "Who am I?" question is answered by the self-sufficient in personal terms: "I am an individual who must make my own way through life and who, in the end, can rely on no one else to get me through difficulties."

How did we identify and develop this classification? As will be seen, there were collaborators who just did not fit the resource-based pattern. When asked to whom they turned for help and advice, their quick and sure answer was "No one!" And their stories were consistent with the answer.

The circumstances varied and their histories were each unique, but their certainty that they were fundamentally on their own was consistent and authentic.

Are the self-sufficients unhappy in their chosen coping style? Not really. Partly because they are not that alone; self-sufficients may be in regular interaction with others. Partly because they gain satisfaction from their independence and self-reliance. In fact, we located a number of older women who define that epitome of dependence, the "old folks home," as an instrument of independence. Self-sufficiency is not social isolation. These people are not bereft of associations; they just do not place ultimate reliance in their relationships.

Who Are the Self-Sufficient?

These independent people are not a demographically representative sample of the entire number of those interviewed. Of the 14, twelve are women, five have been divorced at least once, five are widowed, five are over 80, and ten are retired. They are also disproportionately of the two life course types with disruptions: seven zigzag and three turning point types. Together with the accepting adaptors and resistant rebels, they make up 31% of the 120 who were intensively interviewed.

Most noteworthy is the large number of women. In fact, the two men who are self-sufficients are hardly typical: one has been married four times and the other was so withdrawn that his interview is probably the least informative of the entire number. Rather, the modal self-sufficient is a woman who has had a history of self-reliance and often some early failure of "normal" sources of security.

Social Origins of the Self-Sufficient

What follows is not an argument that there are no psychological factors in the development of self-sufficiency. No doubt there are personal predispositions, what are non-technically called "personality factors," in shaping response patterns. Faced with much the same traumas and deprivations, some become quite independent and others seek the strength of associations with others all the more. Further, there are strains of self-sufficiency in some who are also invested in a pattern of balance or even family-focus. Nevertheless, we did find some striking patterns common to many in this category.

First, the fact that twelve were women indicates that some sort of gender factor is operative. Our small sample cannot yield definitive identification of the relative weight of opportunity deprivations, socialization biases, and possible genetic differences. We can point to the histories of our informants: of the twelve women, at least eight had some major disruption or deprivation in their lives before or during midlife. Four had been divorced, five widowed, and several had some element of marital separation in their stories. From age cohorts in which the norm for women was to be dependent on men, they had found that independence was an alternative course.

Second, that lack of security in dependence was for some reinforced by an ideology of independence. A fear or failure of dependency may have been interpreted through a positive value placed on self-sufficiency. Just how a resistance to being dependent combines with a desire to be independent remains an unresolved question. That the self-sufficient style includes those who have learned this combination in their own histories seems clear.

Factor 1: Early Disruption of Relationships

Marian had been married ten years when she divorced a husband who stole to provide for himself. One of her four children died at ten months. After the divorce she raised the six-year-old middle child and surrendered the others to her husband. After five years she married again, this time to a career Army man with whom she moved from place to place. After her divorce she had "always worked" in retail stores until moving back to Peoria when her husband left the service. He died seven years later in 1978 following a long illness. In recounting the divorce, loss of children, and second husband's death, she repeated that each had made her "a stronger person." After being widowed, "I had to live for me. There was no one else to do it." Later she had open heart surgery and realized that she was alone. When feeling low, "I do something, keep busy, go somewhere." "When you're alone, you learn to take care of you." Now, after five more heart surgeries, this 69-year-old woman has relied on the skill of doctors and nurses and appreciates some support from her brother. Her children are scattered. She reads, watches a lot of television, and goes out to eat at least twice a week with a neighbor/friend. When she was widowed relatively early, married friends dropped her and she had to find new companions. She has a very limited income as well as precarious health. She likes to help others even though she says she is "not a joiner." Her story is one of serial losses in which she has been thrown more and more on her own resources. She says she likes herself and has gained in strength through each trauma and loss. She has learned self-sufficiency when one-by-one so many common sources of support were lost.

Another woman, now 63, was divorced twice by the time she was 18. Her independence was partly a response to the failure of these attempts at conventional relationships, but was later accentuated by her adoption of a lesbian life style. For a man who was married for the fourth time in his late fifties, the family context of investment and support had also not worked out well.

Al's first wife had been "stepping out" before divorcing him and leaving him with the children. His second wife "ran off with the minister." His third wife "slipped me a mickey in a bar," got him to a minister for a quick wedding, and "that's all I remember." Not surprisingly, she left after two years with some financial reward for her time. Despite the fifteen years of his fourth marriage, such a series of betrayals has left him reluctant to rely fully on others. His series of jobs was terminated when Caterpillar "gave me the boot" when he reached age 65. Now he has been told he has Parkinson's disease in addition to his fourteen years of diabetes and a heart condition. He works a lot around the house and yard along with some helpful neighbors and enjoys their children who are "like grandchildren" to him. His life style seems to be mostly alone in his projects, partly because his wife has polio and brittle bones that result in frequent hospitalization and limit her activity outside the home. In all this, his biggest loss came when his three children went back to their mother (his first wife) after his second wife left him. Then his second wife sued for custody of their son, won, and disappeared. When their son was twelve, Al found them, was denied visiting rights, and lost contact again. He stills holds on to an ice-cream-stained shirt that is "all I've got of my memories."

Marian and Al illustrate all too well how a series of failed relationships can culminate in a view of life that excludes others as fully reliable sources of support and meaning. It should be emphasized, however, that such self-sufficient individuals do not necessarily cut off from others. Al has a fourth marriage of 15 years going, cares for his wife, and interacts in mutual assistance with his neighbors. Marian raised three children and cared for her husband through his terminal illness. The lack of community roots due to moving so often and her children's distance are other factors in a lack of cohesive relationships with others. Neither Al nor Marian are isolated or lack concern for others. Yet, somehow they have come to define themselves as essentially self-sufficient and unable to count on others when life's impacts hit home.

Factor 2: A Lack of Investment Security: Al certainly found that he could not count on intimate others. Some dimension of such a failure in relationships is found in many of the stories of the self-sufficient. Of course, we have no sure way of ascertaining the extent to which Al demonstrated characteristics that were reciprocal to such betrayal. His behavior toward his wives may have precipitated some of the failure of trust and intimacy. His "learning" to be independent may have been built on some predispositions and defenses against real sharing.

For a 68-year-old secretary, the failure of marriage to provide a full context for sharing and investment is less repetitive. She found a job in a small insurance company after being divorced at age 32. She was the single parent of two sons and one daughter, all three of whom are now out on their own with their own families. At the time of the divorce, she "decided to make it. I am a very strong and determined person." Now she is proud that her children are independent and doing well. "I did it by myself," she asserts. She has been careful not to get too involved with workmates at her company. She is planning to do more sewing when she retires in two years. She divides life into before and after 1950, the year of her divorce. She is the seventh of eight children from a sturdy family stock. She and her younger brother are close, and she attributes much of her strength to family solidarity as well as to her religious faith. It was the theme of independence, however, that recurred over and over in the interview. When life turned upside down due to the divorce, she assessed her strength, found it adequate to the tasks, and went ahead to manage her life and raise her children to be independent.

The increased number of single-parent, employed women in our society today suggests that such self-sufficiency may become a more common coping style. When the traditional supports and investment contexts fail, one response is to learn a negative lesson—that you can't rely on others—and go it alone. Again, it is important to recognize that we are not talking about isolates who cut off from others and burrow into their anti-social shelters. Rather, like the woman just described, self-sufficients fully accept family responsibilities and take satisfaction in completing them. They work with others and often join churches and other organizations. What distinguishes them is a kind of carefulness or reserve about counting on others. They may be with others in interaction, responsible roles, and even helping modes. But when it comes to their own lives, they find their fundamental resources within themselves.

Winnie became the breadwinner when her husband's health failed. Now retired just a few months from being director of volunteer services at a hospital, she still has open house and open kitchen for her launched children. It hasn't been easy. After the initial period of trying to do it all, she reached a point of exhaustion and had to quit working for a period. Soon, however, she found a better job and has been employed up to her retirement. Since she had to maintain a front of enthusiasm with the volunteers, she often slipped away onto a country road to be alone and eat lunch in peace. The pressures of the job were shared with no one, not even her husband whose work had been more manual. Winnie felt that the stress of her life had been more a condition than a matter of specific circumstances. The pressures of the job, the financial responsibility, trying to "make it up to the children" when she was home from work, and simply being the responsible one made up a heavy and continual load. The year of exhaustion was frightening. When her own health was threatened and she had a hysterectomy, she was able to regain her strength and enthusiasm by sheer determination. Who helped? No one really, certainly not her husband who was ill and 14 years older. She did have a close woman friend, but had time to be with her only about once a month. Like others in this category, now that her children are launched, her leisure is mostly alone: reading, walking, some handwork, and driving to the country. She is, however, involved with her grown children in informal exchange. She likes to be alone and feels free then. Winnie has had a lot of pressure and taken a lot of responsibility. She feels the load and hopes to spend more time with her grandchildren now, perhaps to discover a new style of relaxed interaction. She has had neither the time nor interest for organizations that seemed "shallow" in the midst of her pressures. From one perspective, Winnie lived for others, but in a very self-sufficient mode.

After all, when a person really is on her own, she is likely to develop a definition of her life that corresponds to that reality. When she makes it, she is likely to give herself the credit. "I did it!" may be a realistic assessment rather than an ungrounded boast.

Lois is a younger woman, age 50, whose husband has gone to Texas to find a job. Her current independence seems more a culmination of a pattern than a sudden loss. He has been gone more than at home for seven years. There have been several deaths in her family and her daughter has had four serious eye surgeries. She believes that she is a strong person and has had to be to raise a son and daughter without help from her husband. She used to get some support from her mother and stepfather, but now has only a sister-in-law left. Running a day care center in her home is demanding, but not as physically demanding as her former janitorial position. For leisure, she works in the garden, walks, listens to music, putters around the house, watches TV soaps, and misses the fishing she used to do. She used to be involved in helping with Meals on Wheels and some neighborhood charitable drives. Lois likes to help others and is still active in the neighborhood. Her independence is more a default than for some who are more militantly self-sufficient. She misses the family members who have died, communicates a sense of loneliness, and likes to work with other people. But, she is on her own and has recognized that reality. Some of the support and investment opportunities that have given balance for others just have not been there for this woman who is likely to find her responsibilities for her daughter continuing and her abilities increasingly limited by her spinal arthritis.

Factor 3: Self-Sufficiency as an Ideology: How much independence is a response to failures in support and investment and how much a chosen life definition? In none of our cases could we separate out an ideology of independence from the circumstances of the life course. Nevertheless, there does seem to be more than acceptance and resignation involved here.

Perhaps the most dramatic suggestion of an ideology of independence was found in a surprising place, three "old folks" homes. We interviewed there women ages 83, 84, 85, and 86. Along with another woman of 81 years who is in her own home, they reiterated litanies of independence. One theme in gerontological literature is that intermediate care facilities foster dependence, partly by institutional necessity and partly due to administrative convenience. They are alleged to encourage passivity and are even accused of employing tranquilizers to ease their own workloads. No doubt such institutions exist. But we found something else, a little set of resistant women who had chosen viable homes for older people so they would not be dependent on others. They were proud that their decision had freed their children from the obligation to take care of them. They were independent because they were in a care institution and were proud of it.

For the four in such homes, there are a number of common dimensions:

1. They had chosen to enter such homes. They were not "placed" there.
2. They were in facilities that fostered some activity and engagement.
3. They had the social resources to interact with others.
4. They had lived active lives.
5. They hated the very idea of "being a burden" on anyone else, even their children.
6. They had been caretakers for others.

On the other hand, no two stories or set of circumstances were alike. The youngest, only 83, was widowed only two years ago. Her husband, however, had been paralyzed for eight years following a surgical error.

When he died, she moved back to Peoria from Arizona at her daughter's insistence, but didn't want to be a burden. So she moved into the home which she believes offers both independence and security. She likes to get out, enjoys music, jokes with the other residents, talks to her sister on the phone, and enjoys visits with her daughter and her family. But she doesn't want anyone else to endure what she went through with her husband. She remembers the earlier good times, but also the despair and agony. To whom does she turn for help? "Nobody!" She has memories and mementos, is making new friends, and stays in touch with her family. But she is dependent on no individual but herself!

The 84-year-old also hates the very idea of being dependent. She was married after entering the retirement home to a man of some wealth. They did a lot of travelling before his death. Now she is left secure financially, but cannot travel independently because of a vision impairment. A retired teacher of mentally retarded children, she now reads through talking books. She still travels some by paying the way of a companion and contributes heavily to a small church. The "endowment" from her late-life husband has enabled her to purchase independence.

The woman of 85 is also adamantly independent. She is quite frail, cannot see well, and misses all the bridge games that occupied her for years. Divorced early, she raised one daughter who is now in New Mexico. She prefers her room at the end of a hall because of its relative privacy. She was employed in retail sales for a number of years while living with another woman. When she died after their 21 years of shared residence, our collaborator moved to the retirement home. She supports her daughter's independence, talks to her every Saturday on the phone, and at the same time is very aware of the distance between them. Her eye disease has cost her the possibility of sustained reading or watching television. She is worried about both blindness and financial hardship. Nevertheless, she does not want to trade dependence on the institution for dependence on her daughter.

The 86-year-old widow is a retired county nurse who had been very active when younger. Without children of her own, she cared for a widowed and ill brother and her diabetic husband, worked as a nurse, and helped a divorced brother. When she was finally free of such responsibilities, she became more active in religious organizations and began travelling with groups of retirees. Like the others, she has experienced so much caring for others that she is aware of the problem and does not want to become dependent on others.

The fifth woman in ther 80s remains in her own home, but is similar in her orientation toward independence. Her daughters are married. She was widowed six years ago after a long period of care necessitated by her husband's illness. She wants to manage her own finances and home. For leisure she is in a bridge club, gardens, reads, and visits her extended family. She is sure that they are ready to help when needed, but her greatest fear is becoming dependent. And she misses a male friend who died recently because he shared her independent values and, like her, was more likely to help others than want help for himself. She believes that people need more "fight" so they can avoid becoming dependent on others.

Note again that these women had experienced the strain and constraints of having others dependent on them. Not wanting to inflict that on anyone else, especially their children who had their own lives to live, they had made decisions that would allow them to be independent. Further, they were very satisfied with their decisions. In fact, one described herself as a "self-satisfied old woman." By this she seemed to mean that she had arranged her life to correspond with her values.

Where does this ideology come from? If the exemplars were a group of Montana ranchers or masculine-oriented males, we would have no difficulty in pointing out the male socialization patterns of rugged individualism. However, these women were the ones who had taken care of those males who had become dependent. Perhaps they had experienced the conflict in those men. Certainly they had experienced the stress and constraints on their own lives and did not want to inflict that on others. And, women, too, in a culture that values independence may learn the value and apply it to their own circumstances. Whatever the etiology of the avoidance of dependence, the idea that the old folks home may be defined as a place of independence is startling enough to jar some stereotypes.

Factor 4: Individual Differences: Whatever attention we may give to factors of personal history, social insecurities, and ideologies of independence, there are also some idiosyncratic cases. They remind us that we should never fail to recognize that some individuals have special circumstances that make a critical difference.

One woman in our sample seems more withdrawn than other self-sufficients. She has a hip malformation that has affected her entire life. For a time her mobility was improved by a surgical procedure, but in time the crippling returned. She raised three children, has "few close friends," has engaged in some home crafts, and believes that she has lived a "dull life." The truth is that she has concentrated on her family, stayed home, and accepted her limitations. Perhaps she is "self-contained" more than self-sufficient. There are also the themes of acceptance and family-focus. Yet, she has been engaged with life in a relatively close circle, does not express dissatisfaction with her life, and looks out for herself in her somewhat enclosed environment.

Another less consistent theme is expressed by those who refer to themselves as "loners." Two subjects, the withdrawn man and the retired nurse, used the term in self-definition. Others made similar references.

Again, there may be something of a continuum here with "loners" at one extreme and "engaged self-sufficients" at the other. Some who are independent seem to want to be only minimally connected with others. Others have been quite involved on a series of roles and responsibilities. They are not avoiding engagement and have often been quite active in helping others. They do, however, have a central quality of self-sufficiency and are sure they never want to be dependent on others. Call it "individual difference" or call it personality. There are consistent ways of defining life and the self that cannot always be accounted for by personal histories of either the failure of others or the strain of having others dependent on them.

The Locus of Resources

The life course is seldom fully "under control." In listening to these stories and analyzing their commonalities, we cannot help but be aware that "things happen that make a difference." We do not totally shape the circumstances of our lives, no matter how existential we may be. In our analysis, the critical dimension may not be "locus of control" as much as "locus of resources." The self-sufficients have found that they can rely most fully only on themselves.

These people are not failures, but have coped with change reasonably well. They have found strength within themselves. Some were turned inward by the failure of others or the loss of external sources of support and aid. Others were cut off from the reciprocity of central roles by death, illness, or betrayal of significant others. And some came to believe that independence was an achievement of which they could be proud. Yet, there is something more. Where did they locate their inner strength?

Some learned by making it—day by day and year by year. Finding themselves in sequences of circumstances in which they had to make it for themselves and for those dependent on them, they turned inward and found the strength required. They seem to have been capable of more reciprocity in their roles than they were able to demonstrate. Like Marian after her divorce or Winnie when she had to take over family support, they did what had to be done and developed independence and strength in the process. They didn't set out to be self-sufficient as much as they discovered inner resources in the course of doing what had to be done.

Religion as a Source of Help

Religion was an important factor for some. Their religion, however, was not oriented primarily toward the church as community. The most dramatic example is the woman who developed a lesbian life style after two very early divorces. Her religion was one of meditation rather than community. She had taken lessons and obtained literature from many of the popular self-awareness cults of the 50s and 60s: Science of Mind, EST, Unity, Silva Mind Culture and others. These organizations offer training sessions as well as literature, but their primary practice is solitary and meditative. They foster turning inward and finding strength in practices of meditation and reformulation of self-definitions. They are, then, well suited to persons who have become essentially self-sufficient.

The others who referred to religion as a source of strength ranged from rather vague assertions that "faith in God helped" to more conventional association with mainline churches. In all cases, the self-sufficient contrasted with faithful members who found primary support in the *people* of the church community. Rather, self-sufficients believed that personal religion gave them strength to be independent and to cope with problems. On the other hand, unlike the accepting adaptors who will be analyzed in the next chapter, they were unlikely to explain their troubles as given to them by God.

How Well Did They Cope?

What about success? How well did the self-sufficients do in coping with later-life change? On the life satisfaction scale, they spread out across the spectrum: 1 very high, 8 high, and 2 in each of the three lowest levels. We would not expect them to have the same levels of subjective well-being as those who are closely and securely integrated into immediate communities. And they do not. On the other hand, two-thirds of them have done reasonably well in coping with life courses that present a number of difficulties and deprivations. We might argue that it is still better to make the journey with others, but that it can be done in a more solitary fashion. It is more satisfying to share, both joys and troubles. Yet, most of these individuals learned to take care of themselves and even care for others with a minimum of social support. They found enough inner strength, sometimes from their own families of origin, to do what had to be done. Most also had tried to teach some self-sufficiency to their children. It would be interesting to study the long-term results of that mode of socialization.

Leisure Styles

One striking dimension of the lives of the self-sufficients was their preference for leisure done alone. Winnie's driving off to country roads to be alone for lunch was unique, but the number who listed reading, walking, and hobbies usually done at home as among their three most significant leisure activities was noteworthy. Of the 39 total possible responses for 13 people, 6 chose reading, 5 gardening, 5 television, and 2 each walking, listening to music, or fishing in contrast to the 5 who selected the usually most important category of being with family and friends, and 6 who chose the social activities of religion, travel, or voluntary organizations. Again, the self-sufficient are not social isolates, but they tend to rely on themselves, even in their leisure. In the leisure domain, too, they are more self-contained.

Other Questions

These people are independent but not isolated, contained but not cut off. Several have responded to failures in community and intimacy by seeking their resources within themselves. They have neither given up nor retreated from their responsibilities. Many have continued to find satisfaction in helping others. However, they do not expect reciprocity. Their giving is not done in anticipation of equal receiving. They work, raise children, and even support community organizations and try to be good neighbors. Sometimes they seek advice as one part of coping. But they are independent in the way they define themselves and their sources of support and strength. They captain their own craft, however small and frail it may become in later years.

We might speculate on the future life orientations of the greatly increasing number of women who like some of the self-sufficient have been single-parent breadwinners. Will the style of self-containment become more and more common for women or will the fact that they are more numerous stimulate more opportunities for social support and integration?

We might also speculate on the influence of old-style American individualism on the underlying ideology of independence. If most of the self-sufficient were not women, then some suggestion about rugged individualism and the frontier ethos would be almost inevitable. Since the pattern is not a masculine one, then it seems more a positive response to a failure in traditional gender role definitions and reciprocity. These women have found themselves in a set of life conditions in which dependence on males was not a viable option.

Their positive style of responsible independence suggests a final speculation. They did not withdraw in the face of challenge, but developed their own resources to cope and in some cases to overcome. They were not passive, but took a more existential view of their lives. If life was to go on—for themselves and sometimes for their families—they had to take action. What is distinctly different here is the extent to which they then took a somewhat existential view of life. They had to do it because there was no one else. In the end, no matter how many people show concern and even care, there is no one to truly share the responsibility for life. They believe that in the end, we are each responsible for our own lives. We cannot and should not rely finally on any others.

Although the term "loners" was used in self-description by two or three, most were "helpers." They had experienced the woman's lot of caretaking, sometimes in multiples and sequences. They were not cut off, just independent. They took responsibility for their own lives and when necessary for others. But they learned to rely on themselves and defined themselves as alone. No two are just alike, in history or definitions of themselves or their live contexts. Yet, there are the persistent themes of self-containment and of responsible independence. They do not invest in others.

6
Accepting Adaptors
and Resistant Rebels

A s early interviews were reviewed, the verb "accept" was heard over and over. "How did you cope with this change?" "I just had to accept it" was a common response. One variation was added to the acceptance theme: "I did what I had to do." The responses, however, indicated that all adapted to the trauma. Further, this acceptance and adaptation were described as though there were no alternatives.

The "accepting adaptor", then, is a person whose coping style is a personal acceptance of the event and its ramifications. Imagine a health trauma that destroys the entire fabric of economic support and family responsibilities: the response is to accept it—generally without complaint—and make whatever changes are necessary to go on. And, as we will see, those who exhibit this style generally have some other factors in common as well. One such accepting adaptor has had her life taken over by the requirements of caring for her husband.

> Elizabeth says it is her duty to accept whatever comes and to "do what God wants." She worked for years in a nursing home. Now she has to care for her husband who suffers from a degenerative disease of the joints and nervous system that left him unable to move from place to place. So, Elizabeth, 76 years old herself and with high blood pressure and arthritis in her knees, has for five years moved, fed, and cared for him. She has to call for help if he swivels and falls, because he cannot lift himself. Living on the edge of town, they do not have access to public transportation and cannot afford taxis. Her husband did not work for Caterpillar long enough to receive a pension. That is why Elizabeth worked 16 years in a nursing home while in her 50s and 60s and then for several years part-time to try to make ends meet.
>
> Her history is one of deprivation and marginality from the beginning. In their early married years, she and her husband had a little subsistence farm in southern Illinois. He also worked in the

strip mines to provide some income. In time the mines destroyed the farmland so he found factory work. A series of illnesses, layoffs, and loss of medical benefits led to scrambling for income. He did odd jobs, garden plowing and handy work, especially after being laid off from Caterpillar at age 65 with no retirement benefits. Elizabeth worked for low pay in a nursing home as long as she could, until his condition required her to be home all the time.

Questions about self-worth mean little to her. "I've never had a chance to think about myself." Her daughter helps out some and grandchildren come in on weekends to give her some relief. Support for her is financial, the household items that their children sometimes buy for them. With only minimum social security and a tiny pension from the nursing home, they try to make ends meet but find that medical costs are becoming overwhelming.

How does she deal with all this? Elizabeth believes that her life is what God wants it to be. It is her obligation to do the best she can with it. "That's just the way life is." She is a caretaker who sees life in that framework. She can't get to church. They can no longer take day trips to visit their children. This year she couldn't even plant her garden and misses that little act of creating something that is her own. She believes that she has fulfilled her "responsibilities in life" and that God is happy with her. She will soon have to place her husband in a nursing home and will need help herself with transportation and medical care. But for now, she continues her superhuman efforts to get through the day and defines her life as caring for those who need her.

Elizabeth has more to cope with than many other accepting adaptors. Her situation may be severe, but it is not unique. Elements in her story are found in the lives of other adaptors as well.

Who Are the Accepting Adaptors?

Those who take this particular approach to the changes in their lives are like the self-sufficient in one significant way: they are disproportionately women. Accepting adaptors are also more religious and passive. Both accepting adaptors and the self-sufficient often lack external resources and rely only on themselves. The difference is the degree to which their internal resources have enabled them to take effective action.

The Gender Factor

Eleven of the 14 accepting adaptors are women. Like self-sufficiency, this style is found mostly among women. The three men who were classified as accepting adaptors had not coped well with their life course.

1. One divorced man, age 57, had his son turn against him after the divorce. His own relationship with his father was a bitter one. Now he claims to enjoy interacting with people in a restaurant where he works, but believes he is a failure because of the family dissolution. He even ponders the possibility that God is angry at him because of this failure.

2. A retired 78-year-old former company representative misses the associations of the road and his sales contacts. His wife, who had been ill most of her life, is dead, and he finds his home and life empty. His own health is failing. His daughters come in regularly. He watches TV and goes out in his little car some. But in general he is just waiting for death and hopes that it will come soon.

3. The most "successful" male adaptor is a black retired worker who is close to his wife and active in his church despite severe financial limitations. He interprets the restrictions in his life course as the life God has assigned him. He copes through "faith in God." Having no children, he is involved with his neighbors. The general tenor of his life, however, is one of passivity rather than reaching out to action that might create change.

For the first two of these men, accepting has overtones of "giving up." There is a "that's the way it is and there isn't anything I can do about it" resignation. For the third, the acceptance is also passive, but the acceptance is less negative due to his marriage and church.

For, the women, on the other hand, acceptance is in the context of female roles and resources. A 63-year-old never-married is relaxed with people. Her life course has been dotted with the deaths of family members and later of a male friend to whom she had been close for 21 years. She misses them, especially at Christmas, but goes on in her quiet routines. She bowls and has monthly lunches with other retired "Cat" women. For the most part, however, she just accepts the changes of retirement and the loss of significant others and goes on.

Another woman of the same age is married and has one daughter who has come back home to live. This woman seems quite inhibited socially, perhaps due to a severe rash she cannot hide. She is not happy, but keeps to herself socially with some home-based hobbies. She also keeps to herself her worry about her daughter, her grief over losing her parents in 1961, and a conflict-ridden marriage. A Catholic of Lebanese ethnic origin, she is passive to the point of withdrawal.

Francis has always been in big families. She had 13 brothers in her childhood. She is the mother of six and the grandmother of thirty. Now 72, she became divorced in 1936 after being married six years. She moved to public housing after the divorce, eventually bought a house, and has now had to move to an apartment. Despite only one year of high school, she was a postal clerk for 23 years and retired at age 62. She has had health problems—diabetes, high blood pressure, and two operations—and is bothered by one daughter's divorce. Extended family is important to Francis. Grandchildren come by every week or so to help out. She visits in the homes of cousins and is with a sister-in-law almost every Sunday. Her affiliation with the Democratic Club and a church do not seem central.

When Francis talks about the large family, it is often in terms of financial requirements—"buying all those shoes." Her story is one of caretaking in a context that has been common for black women whose marriages were short-lived. She had to do it all. She says that she didn't "stay down in the dumps too long" when problems arose. The truth is that she didn't have time. With all her caretaking responsibilities, she "had a life to live." She would talk problems over with someone and then go on. She has been busy in life supporting her children. She was involved with others and coped with difficulties "as best (she) could." There just wasn't time to do more than recognize what had to be done, accept realities, and go ahead.

Francis is one of the most engaged of the accepting adaptors. Yet, her style is one of making do and going on. She talks to others, but also says she is just as comfortable when alone. Her life has been so packed with practical, day-to-day requirements that she has not had the luxury of doing more than accepting them and trying to cope. As a woman, she had the caretaking roles along with the breadwinning required of most divorced women, probably all single women in the lower income segments of the population.

Religion and Acceptance

Nine of the 14 adaptors referred to a religious framework for their interpretation of their lives. Some were active in churches, but just as many were not. Yet, the idea that God is the source of life's events, that there is a divinely ordered set of life circumstances, is a common theme in these stories. Perhaps the source is a pervasive religiosity that extends beyond the direct influence of church institutions. Perhaps the idea of divine order is comforting to many who seem to have little control over their life courses. In any case, for those who tend to accept and go on with little question, a religious vocabulary may be used to "make sense" of the sequence of events that seems so out of control.

The man who was a trustee of his black church demonstrated the most institutional style of coping through the acceptance of support by traditional religion. A 69-year-old widow also goes to church regularly where she sings in the choir. With only grade-school education, she worked as a housekeeper after the store she used to clean went out of business. Now she works only one day a week and has more time for her own knitting and helping older people. She misses her husband who died six years ago. Her life is a "helper" mode, and she appreciates the pastor, her son, and others who have helped her. Her interpretation, however, is one of a religious-based acceptance. "I accept the way things are" is her theme. She doesn't believe in feeling sorry for herself or in sitting home feeling bad. Yet, like other adaptors, she was surprised when asked what gave her a sense of self-worth. That just wasn't an issue for her.

The same vocabulary is common to those who have not had to deal with opportunities limited by racism. "God has given me this life and it is my duty to accept it" picks up the most persistent themes. As people deal with limitations and changes, they may be comforted by the idea that an uncomplaining acceptance is what God wants of them. Some couple this with the hope of a reward in another existence. For others, the religious accounting is a familiar way of stating their accepting posture rather than an articulation of doctrine.

The Passive Voice

The essence of this style is passivity. This does not mean that these people have not acted responsibly to take care of themselves and of others. However, they seem to respond by doing "what had to be done" rather than assessing resources and seeking alternatives. They are quite unreflective as they recount the transitions and traumas that they dealt with.

Now 82, one widow had the educational and social resources that were lacking for in many of the adaptors. The turning point in her life came when her husband, a professor at a major midwest university, died. She had engaged in the full fabric of activities expected in her role as faculty wife. When her husband died, she immediately moved to Peoria at the urging of her brother and sister. Rather than proactively rebuild her life in the resource-rich university town, she left the home where they had lived for 48 years and went into an apartment in a strange town. Role-dependent as well as passive, she says that changes "are just a part of life" as though she had not had options and alternatives. Her health is now quite precarious, but death—also "just a part of life"—does not worry her. Each night she prays to die, but accepts each new day.

The key may be in what adaptors see as the range of possibilities. They are unreflective about what is possible as well as about how their definitions of the situation are a factor in shaping the future. For those with a heavy load of responsibilities and few resources, this attitude is manifested in just doing what has to be done to get through the day or week. For others, acceptance is more a matter of how life is viewed—in a religious or secular "givenness" that just has to be taken as it comes.

Resistant Rebels as an Extreme Type

The other end of an acceptance-resistance continuum is the coping style of the "resistant rebel." This is, of all the styles, the closest to an "ideal type." It seemed that one style of coping would be to fight back, to attempt to change the events or, at least, the environment in which they occurred. A victim of racism would resist politically. A victim of injustice on the job might become a union activist. Someone deprived of education would fight to get back to school or to be self-educated. Resistance would be a matter of defining life's circumstances as unacceptable and acting to change them.

We did find some elements of such resistance, certainly in a balanced investor like Alma and her civil rights activism. But for the most part, the rebel category had no pro-active or directed individuals who refused to accept limitations or restrictions as "givens." Whatever the reasons, those now in their 50s, 60s, 70s, and 80s in Peoria did not learn to fight back. Some probably just didn't have the resources. Others didn't have the inclination. Some invested where there were opportunities. A few defined their lives in terms of a central commitment. Some found resources within themselves or just accepted the limits and went along. But the two "rebels" we located appeared to be problems to themselves more than to others. They were different and resistant, but certainly not agents of social change.

> Evan had a fascinating life story. A "donkey boy" in the mines of Wales before he was ten, he had a long history of struggle and deprivation. He was also a "driver" in the Illinois mines after coming to America as a youth. His succession of jobs culminated in twenty years at Hiram Walker's distillery. When his wife died in 1972, Evan was depressed and lonely. He drank heavily, lost 50 of his 190 pounds, and landed in the hospital. Now that he has stopped drinking, he is cut off from his tavern associates. He is too poor to drink, he says. His style of association is now somewhat bizarre. He is sure that all his neighbors but one are out to get him. He tells of an alleged attempt at poisoning as well as being hit by a car. The one loyal neighbor takes him to the store and to eat out once a week. She is the link with the communicative and caring world for this 87-year-old whose feistiness has turned to bitterness and alienation. Evan is poor, but he is certainly neither accepting nor adapting.

The other man classified as a resistant rebel also had a history of disappointment and alienation. In 1980 his wife died after 39 years of marriage. His children visit and are concerned about his well-being. At his job he was moved aside to make room for the owner's son-in-law. He complained without effect and now registers his resistance by refusing to punch the time clock. He wants to be independent and has encouraged that trait in his children. His daughter paid her own way through college. Now he no longer can play golf with his son who moved out of the park district and refuses to pay the visitor's fee. He believes that he is alone by choice. He lost his wife and two close friends and doesn't want to get that close again. His church involvement ended when he decided that any concern shown him after his wife died was just done as a religious duty. He seems very unsure of his ability to make new friends and pushes others away. His resistance is expressed in little ways, not major campaigns.

It may be that these two men hardly fit the category at all. They resist and blame others for their problems, but in a personal rather than system-blaming mode. Some would just call them "neurotic" or, to use less pejorative terminology, "unadapted." We just didn't find anyone in this type to contrast to passive acceptance by recognizing alienation and fighting back.

Again, the typology lends itself to the formulation of a continuum—this one on an acceptance–resistance dimension as shown in figure 6-1.

This continuum acknowledges the fuzziness in distinguishing between coping types. For example, Francis, the divorced postal clerk with the large extended family, would probably be located on this scale about half way between the self-sufficients and the accepting adaptors. Her success in coping and self-confidence seem on a higher level than most of the adaptors. On the other hand, her vocabulary of accounting is very much in the mode of acceptance.

Typologies inevitably divide up the real world of real people too neatly. Certainly the one developed in this study is no exception. It is a useful framework for analysis and presentation. On the other hand, no two individuals fit within a category in just the same way and with the same unambiguous certainty. The acceptance–resistance continuum is not a dichotomy and certainly not a trichotomy. Further, it is weighted toward the acceptance end with consistent resistance hard to locate. Nevertheless, the dimension points to stylistic differences in both mode of action and of definition.

The Life Histories of Accepting Adaptors

There are two themes evident in the life histories of accepting adaptors. The first is, like self-sufficients, a lack of resources. The second is a world view

Low ———————————————————————————— High

     Resistant Rebels   Self-Sufficients   Accepting Adaptors

Figure 6-1. Degrees of Acceptance

that accepts "given" rather than turns to internal resources. Together they form a stance toward life that does not support effectual action.

Resource Deprivation

One striking item of history was found: among the eleven accepting adaptor women, four had worked as cleaning women and one in a laundry. Several had not finished high school, usually because they had to work to help support their parental family. Others had lost the financial resource of an employed husband due to illness, death, or divorce. There were exceptions, but the common story of these women is one of very limited resources and opportunities.

A 62-year-old widow lost her husband when she was 53 after three years of his incapacitating illness. She worked in a laundry for 22 years until it went out of business and then drew unemployment. She will now receive social security and is looking for part-time work to supplement that income. Left to support most of the eight children when the youngest was nine, she had already been the sole earner in the family for several years. She refers to her independence as well as the need to accept life's events and tasks. How did she deal with this trauma as well as the deaths of parents and a brother? "You adjust yourself. You just do it . . . some way." Her launched children live out of town and can give only occasional telephone support. They visit occasionally. She has a religious attitude, but does not go to church. When reviewing her life, she also has trouble with questions about self-worth: "I don't know, the only thing I have done is raised my family." She has coped, but has not gained confidence in herself in the process. She has, and is, just doing what is necessary to keep her family afloat in a very large and threatening sea.

An older widow is one of the four "cleaning women." She, too, lost her husband when her children were young and had to do something to keep things going. All six are now married, but visit her in the nursing home which she does not often leave since breaking a hip. She is still able to participate in the religious life at the church-sponsored home. She listens to religious music and finds satisfaction in visiting those confined to the home's infirmary. Her room has pictures of children and grandchildren in most available spots. After her husband died and her children left, she "lived on" doing what had to be done with little reflection or resistance.

The image here is one of response to the immediate. What was done was what had to be done. The idea of assessing and determining lines of action seems foreign in situations in which the demands are smothering and the opportunities limited. What effectual action can be taken by someone such as Florence?

Florence's husband is mentally ill; he has been in and out of mental hospitals for the past 18 years. She is now burdened by his release into her care, still unable to function effectively or productively. Her church has helped, emotionally and financially. She cleaned at a nursing home and then a motel before building up a clientele of homes to clean. Now the high unemployment rate in Peoria has had a negative impact on some of her employers. Bills from her own surgery are still coming in to add to the financial impact of her husband's illness. She meets her daughter for lunch regularly and a sister somewhat less often. She can't be as active in the church as she would like because of her work, keeping track of her husband, and because the church is in another town. They lived in that town until their house burned down in 1969. Now she accepts her burdens, goes on working, raises almost half a room of indoor plants, and does what she can.

What kind of alternatives are open to someone like Florence? How would a wise and sympathetic counselor advise her to enrich her life, open up new opportunities, or lessen her own load? It's a struggle just to keep going—in energy or in effort. Financially, she just tries not to get too far behind. "Discretionary income" or discretionary anything would be a meaningless phrase to Florence. Whatever may be the psychological predispositions to acceptance, the life course options for action that will make a difference seem few or totally absent.

The Parallel World View

The lack of resources is paralleled by a definition of life as "given." A secretary who works for Caterpillar has a daughter who has returned home with her two children after her divorce and a husband who retired early because of deafness. At 57, she is somewhat involved in a few organizations including the church, but is more likely to relax at home watching TV most evenings. She believes that "You must learn to accept things and do the best you can."

The man who had been estranged from his son at the time of his own divorce put it in more religious terms. For him, God is a somewhat fearsome father figure who judges as well as tests. All this is confused in his personal history by his own relationship with a father who had been very judgmental and harsh, but was found having an extramarital affair. His religious world view is far more complex than those of the several adaptors who believe that God gives the trials of life.

Whether religious or not, defining life with no alternative to acceptance is tied to the concept of "givenness." This world view is 180 degrees away from an existential interpretation that holds that no limits are final and that life is the consequence of decision, however limited to circumstances. If the essence of life is to accept what is given, then no active decision to do something about the circumstances is possible.

Antecedents and Consequences

As will be analyzed more comprehensively in chapter 9, one antecedent of accepting adaptation seems to be social class. One of the three men had a stable blue collar job and another an erratic work history. Of the eleven women, nine had been required to work—four cleaned houses, one worked in a laundry, one was a secretary, one a postal clerk, one a factory hand, and one worked in a nursing home. All but one of the eleven were at the low end of the income scale, and most experienced real poverty. In later years, just making ends meet and trying to keep up with medical expenses were difficult or impossible.

It may be difficult for those who have "discretionary income"—income in excess of food, shelter, medical care, and other necessary expenses—to have a real feel for such constrictions. It is much easier to talk existentially about life-determining decisions when there are almost always some options about the use of resources. When there are none and when financial resources are below the level of obligation, then acceptance must seem like the only possible response. Social class, in the sense of access to opportunity and resources, is determinative for many accepting adaptors, who have seldom been in a position to assess options and make decisions. Many of the women faced overwhelming responsibilities and few resources except their own direct effort. Without educational or economic resources, they cleaned houses or businesses and then came home to children who were totally dependent on them and their meager incomes. They did what they had to do, day by day, with little sense that there might be any other possibilities. What their social placement did was to lower their horizons and blot out any idea of decisions that might begin a new line of action. Social class is more than economic placement; it determines the parameters of the world we learn to see.

Satisfaction and Success

It is evident that the satisfaction level of accepting adaptors is comparatively low: 53% of accepting adaptors are in the low levels of subjective well-being compared to 40% of the self-sufficient, 21% of the family-focused, and 25% of the balanced investors. Only two AAs are in the highest level—13% compared to 31% of the entire sample. Such a measure, however, is only an indication of the level of coping success.

From one perspective, it can be argued that such acceptance is "functional" for those with such limited life chances. When there are, in reality, no alternatives, then a philosophy of acceptance may be the most adaptive stance possible. If there aren't alternatives, then why complain or rebel? Accept, if possible in a religious mode that sees such acceptance as a divinely ordained duty, and do what must and can be done.

From an alternative perspective, there are always options, however limited and difficult. The system does not work well for many of the poor and ill. Therefore, it may be best to seek some way around, through, or over the system. One of the premises of radical social work or of community organization is that "something can be done." Circumstances are, at least in part, made by people and can be altered by people. Unquestioning acceptance perpetuates the system and its inequities.

We are not in a position to pass any judgment on Francis or Elizabeth or their cohorts. However carefully and sympathetically we may listen, few of us really know what it is like to cope with their life chances day after day. We marvel that they can cope and express as much stability and satisfaction as they do. We can, however, ask a question: how much of a chance did they have? For many in a relatively affluent society, resources snowball as they roll through the life course. We now know that economic change and transfer payments make the correlation between age and poverty almost disappear. Market analysts are showing new interest in the discretionary incomes of adults who have launched their children and the active "young old" who are retired. In all this enthusiasm for the snowballing resources of some in life's second half, we should not forget those whose resources were slim to begin with and are almost nonexistent by the time they are in their 70s.

Part II
Social Factors in Coping

7
The Resource of Leisure

W hat is leisure? Common definitions refer to "time for relaxation" or "time leftover from obligations." References to time, however, are empty of content. In the last 20 years, most definitions have focused on what fills that time, on action or some state of being (Kelly, 1982). Leisure is activity that is chosen for some anticipated experience, an action with meaning rather than simply a void of obligation. Further, seldom have persons in our society completed everything that ought to be done or that others expect. In fact, even for those over 65, time scarcity remains the most significant barrier to desired leisure participation (McGuire et al., 1986.)

Leisure, then, is more accurately understood as action with elements of relative freedom (Roberts, 1978), meaning contained largely within the experience, action that has an existential thrust of becoming (Kelly, 1987) or a withdrawal for renewal (Kleiber, 1985). The life course has been found to be the best framework for analyzing how leisure expresses and develops personal and social identities in the sequences of social roles and their intersections (Rapoport and Rapoport, 1976; Kelly, 1983).

The place of leisure in the lives of older people has received attention since the iandmark Kansas City study of Robert Havighurst (1957), Bernice Neugarten (1968), and their associates in which various forms of leisure were found to be significant elements in the lives of older adults. More recently, Atchley (1976) has studied the functions of leisure in retirement. In a study in Houston, Gordon et al. (1976) found that expressive activity remained important to adults through the later life course. Perhaps most compelling has been Palmore's (1979) longitudinal analysis documenting that later-life adaptation is strongly related to activity and social contexts outside the home.

Underlying the analysis is the premise that leisure is more than activity that fills leftover time. Rather, leisure is better understood in a life-course perspective as a multidimensional set of activities, relationships, contexts, and commitments (Kelly, 1983). The interests and choices of leisure are not fixed at some point in the life course but are related to both role sequences and developmental preoccupations. Leisure has two main dimensions: the existential development of life's meanings and the social dimension of providing a context for interaction with significant others (Kelly, 1987).

Leisure, then, could contribute to coping with change in later life in several ways. First, it might simply fill time left open due to the losses that accompany second-half role sequences. When children are launched, work roles reduced or lost, and primary relationships ended by decision or death, leisure can be employed to fill the time void. Social gerontologists have indeed found that participation in nonwork activities is associated with greater satisfaction in later life (Lemon et al., 1972; Peppers, 1977). Second, considerable research has demonstrated that the leisure most valued by adults either involves interaction with important others or is expressive activity in which they have invested considerable effort in gaining competence (Kelly, 1983). For later life adults, this suggests two primary ways in which leisure may contribute:

1. It may be a context for inaugurating, developing, and expressing important social relationships. In this way, leisure's contribution to coping with change would be indirect, through social integration.
2. Leisure may make a more direct contribution in providing possibilities for action that demonstrate and enhance self-definitions of worth and competence. In leisure, we may express and build satisfying indentities.

The first question, then, is "Does leisure make a significant contribution to a satisfying later adult life?" The second question follows: "If so, then how is that contribution made?" To answer both questions, we will summarize statistical analysis of the telephone survey of 400 Peoria adults as well as the 120 intensive household interviews.

Leisure and Life Satisfaction

A recent meta-analysis of 556 sources of data on the relationship of adult social activity and subjective well-being found that formal and informal activity together account for only 1 to 9% of net variance in self-reported life satisfaction (Okun et al., 1984). Further, the types of activity engaged in were not consistently related to satisfaction. At most, there is the implication that such activity is only one of several factors in developing a satisfying adult life.

Therefore, our design was intended to examine leisure as more than time devoted to nonwork activity. Rather, the focus was on the possibility that leisure might be a context for meaningful action and social integration.

Meanings of leisure engagement were examined together with their form and content.

The Telephone Survey

The protocol for the brief telephone interviews with 400 adults age 40 and over randomly selected from the area phone directory included demographic items, range and frequency of leisure activity, a life satisfaction scale, measures of perceived life deficits and problems, and the scope and frequency of interaction with friends and family. The Life Satisfaction Scale (LSI) consisted of six items from a factor-analyzed modification of the LSI (Neugarten et al., 1961) that has been used extensively with older adults (Longino and Kart, 1982). Leisure activity was measured on a four-point scale (never, seldom, occasional, and frequent) for 28 kinds of activities found in previous research to be most typical for older adults (Kelly, 1978). A factor analysis reduced the activities to eight subsets: cultural, travel, home-based, sport-exercise, family, outdoor, community organization, and social activities.

Does leisure contribute to later life satisfaction as measured by the modified LSI? In the analysis, stepwise multiple regression was employed with possible confounding variables entered first in order of their contribution. Together these variables accounted for 11.8% of the variance. They were, in order with Beta weights parenthesized: health (−.236), marital status (.124), age (−.005), education level (−.003), sex (.064), and occupation level (.004). When level of leisure activity was entered, it accounted for an additional 6.2% of the variance after indices of resources and abilities were entered. The Beta of .251 was the highest of all variables. When leisure was included in order of contribution to subjective well-being, it entered first and accounted for 13.3% of the variance with all remaining variables accounting for an additional 7.7%.

This result is in the upper range of those found in the meta-analysis and is consistent with other research. Engagement with leisure activity—both range and frequency—does make a significant contribution to perceived well-being for second half adults. The next question, then, is how.

In this study, there were two ways of approaching this question. One focused on the types of activities that were found to contribute most to satisfaction. The second focused on the meaning of those activities to the participants.

Types of Activities. Based on previous research with adults, the expectation was that two kinds of activity would distinguish those with the highest levels of life satisfaction: those providing a context for interaction with valued others and "high-investment" activities. High-investment activities are those that have been developed over a period of time, require some acquisition of skill, and are most likely to yield outcomes of an enhanced sense of competence, worth, and personal expression.

Many of the activities that afford contexts for interaction fall into the "core" of accessible leisure that continues through most of the life course: informal interaction with household members and friends, shopping, walking, and playing with children, or watching TV and reading. Such activities are frequently home-based and might be expected to persist throughout the life span. High-investment activities, on the other hand, often call for special locales, associates, equipment, and high levels of effort and skill. They may be more difficult for older persons, especially those moving into the final life period of frailty and limitation.

First, the relative rates of participation were calculated. They are displayed in figure 7–1.

Exercise (including sports) and outdoor activity have much lower rates of participation for each older age category. Cultural, travel, and home-based activity are markedly lower only for those age 75 and over. Family activities were slightly lower only for older widows. Social activity was a little higher for men over 75 and lower only for women over 75. Social, home-based, and family activity were the most common for all the over-40 sample with participation in community organizations least frequent.

The low rates of participation in exercise and sport and outdoor recreation for those age 55 and above reflect the likelihood that some health and physical ability factors are operative. This was confirmed in the stories of men who had relinquished their competitive team sport engagement in their 40s as well as those who had quit hunting or fishing when their children were grown and moved away. The overall pattern suggests that there is a common geographical and social constriction of engagement in the later-life course. Especially for those entering or in the final period of "frailty," social contexts come to be limited to family and neighbors while locales of activity center more and more around the residence. The requirements for so much leisure—access, mobility, physical and communicative abilities, and available companions—become more and more limited in the final years.

For our purposes, however, an analysis of which kinds of activities contribute most to life satisfaction for the four age groups is more salient. Cross-tabulations of life satisfaction with participation levels for each type of activity reinforced both the constriction and social context factors. Gamma measures of correlation were employed along with Chi square as a measure of statistical significance. The activity types most strongly associated with high levels of satisfaction are reported in table 7–1.

Community organization participation is negatively related to life satisfaction up to the age of 75. For those 75 and over, there is a modest but

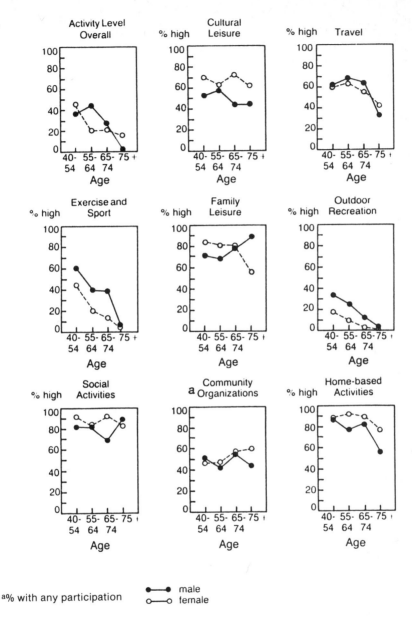

a% with any participation   ●——● male
                                 ○——○ female

Figure 7–1. High Levels of Activity by Age

significant correlation (.214*). While such cross-sectional data must be interpreted without imputing longitudinal change, the analysis is consistent with the case histories:

Table 7–1

Life Satisfaction and Activity Type by Age

Age	Activity Types associated with High Satisfaction
40–54	Cultural (.484**) and Travel (.426**)
55–64	Social (.355), Travel (.336), and Cultural (.311)
65–74	Social (.514*), Travel (.501*), and Cultural (.425)
75+	Home-based (.476), Family (.455), and Cultural (321*)

Source: Kelly, et al., 1987.
Gama measures:
  *PL.05.
  **PL.001

1. Geographical and social constriction is evident only for those most likely to be in frail health. Home-based activities such as hobbies, gardening, and improving things distinguish those with higher satisfaction only in the 75+ age group. Also, the family is the most important set of social relationships.

2. For those under 75, the distinguishing kinds of activity are those that mark a more active and invested life style as well as greater financial resources: travel and cultural activity.

3. Social activities such as entertaining at home, eating out, and various forms of conversation are especially important for those most likely to have launched their children and yet be active—the pre- and post-retirement adults age 55 to 74.

4. Studies of travel invariably point to the significance of the social component ("companionship") in satisfaction with the experience. Travel is one context for the expression of primary relationships.

Leisure as a context for social interaction is highlighted in this analysis. Those who report the highest levels of life satisfaction are those most likely to be actively engaged with significant others in activity that provides stimulation and interaction enrichment. On the other hand, the physical activity and organizational involvement found by Palmore (1979) to contribute to later-life adaptation are not found to be important in this study. Perhaps the rates of participation are just too low to yield significance for the sample of 400. Clearly supported, however, is the pattern of life-course alterations in resources and social contexts related to social role sequences.

Persistent Leisure Orientations. Another way of approaching the question of how leisure contributes to later life satisfaction is in terms of the meanings to the participants. Using a simple scale developed in previous research (Kelly, 1978), the meanings or satisfactions of the two activities considered most important by each respondent were investigated. The 21 short statements with 5-point agree-disagree responses were factor analyzed and yielded the following clusters of meaning: companionship in the activity, strengthening primary relationships, competence and skill-development, expression and personal development, health and exercise, meeting role expectations, and general enjoyment (Kelly et al., 1986). Since role expectations were seldom rated as salient and enjoyment almost always was, only the other five orientations were included in cross-tabulations for the 400 in the telephone sample. Table 7–2 displays the results.

Gender differences are consistent with previous research. Men place more emphasis on health and exercise, companionship, and competence. When analyzed by age, the following tendencies are evident:

1. The social emphasis on primary relationships is higher for men in the post-retirement periods than for those more likely to be in work environments.

2. Competence and skill-development as well as concern for health and exercise are markedly lower for those in the age category of 75 and over.

3. On the other hand, expressing and strengthening primary relationships and personal expression remain high for both men and women throughout the life course.

Leisure satisfactions are multiple and varied. There is no one-to-one correspondence between any activity type and a single dimension of meaning. Some leisure is directed toward the self in expression and development.

Table 7–2
Reasons for Leisure Engagement by Age and Gender

	% High on Each Type of Reason				
Age	Companion-ship	Primary Relations	Competence	Expression	Health/ Exercise
Males					
40–54	58.7	62.0	56.2	65.3	47.1
55–64	49.1	56.6	52.8	56.6	45.3
65–74	63.9	72.2	66.7	69.4	55.6
75+	33.3	75.0	33.3	66.7	41.7
All	55.9	63.1	55.9	64.0	47.7
Females					
40–54	37.7	60.3	44.4	63.6	37.7
55–64	56.1	54.7	48.0	65.5	36.5
65–74	50.5	60.2	52.4	66.0	43.7
75+	44.7	63.8	38.3	68.1	27.7
All	47.7	68.8	46.8	65.3	37.6

Other leisure is more social in nature with particular stress on primary relationships, family, and friends. Leisure is both existential in being chosen with an aim of "becoming" and social in building and expressing significant relationships (Kelly, 1987). In these dual orientations, leisure usually fits into the resources and role expectations that shift through the life course.

From the analysis of the 400 telephone interviews, we learn the following:

1. The social bonding dimension of leisure is primary.
2. Leisure is more than filling time. It is a context for action and interaction that is important to overall life satisfaction.
3. Those who can still travel and initiate activity are least in need of programmatic attention. The oldest group, however, is most limited in geographical and social range in this period when both abilities and resources tend to be diminished. They are most likely to be cut off from the opportunities found most helpful by preretirement and active retirement adults.

The 120: Leisure in Their Stories

The research design employed telephone interviews to provide a kind of map of the territory of over-40 adults in Peoria. Then the 120 collaborative interviews were to fill in the gaps, to provide substantive content to the outline offered by statistical analysis of the behavioral and attitudinal scales of the larger sample. Because of the focus on leisure and social integration, the analysis of the 400 is most complete in these areas. There is, however, considerable richness that is afforded by returning to the cases of the 120.

The core and balance of leisure is demonstrated by the concentrations and varieties of leisure engagements. Leisure choices are not random, but together make up a leisure style that generally fits the overall life style. Leisure is a part of life's orientations and aims, resources and responsibilities. Emily, for example, is the retired schoolteacher who travels with her "best friend" husband to Florida each winter (chapter 2). When in Peoria she sings in a community chorus, goes to plays and concerts, and plays some golf and bridge. Leisure in both locales is a context for making friends and being with people she and her husband enjoy. Travel has components of visiting children, enjoying the warmer climate and the activities it affords in winter, and using the activities to make new friends. Leisure has a social shape of a double circle with marriage at the center of each and other relationships clustered around in the Illinois and Florida activity investments. Emily's leisure has continuity in both associations and activities despite the removal of the work context and the addition of the Florida winter location.

Resources of all kinds are important. The balanced investors were most likely to have attended college, have higher level occupations, and not have experienced a trauma involving major loss. They were also most likely to have a high level of leisure activity and of life satisfaction. For them leisure tended to be a significant area of investment, integrated with, rather than separate from, their other investment domains. Both the conventional and the more highly committed investors developed leisure styles that complemented their work and family roles as well as employed the resources afforded by those roles. Even those with zigzag or turning point life courses dealt with unanticipated changes from a fuller resource base. Leisure both provided and utilized those resources.

The never-married balanced investor who had been retired for a decade from her teaching and librarian positions exemplified the constriction pattern (chapter 2). While working she had engaged in considerable travel and been active in professional and cultural organizations. Now, with her vision failing and her financial resources quite limited, she finds that her circle of associations is largely restricted to the retirement home, its associations, and its media entertainment. Hers is only one story of how reduced abilities and resources combine to make smaller and smaller the circle of activities and associations. The life course has its periods of expansion during its first half: entering school, leaving school, establishing a family, and seeking new opportunities. The second half also may offer expansion when time and financial resources are coupled with lessened obligations during the postparental and early retirement periods. As will be emphasized in chapter 9, for some people resources and opportunities never open up. For most, on the other hand, constriction, however inexorable, comes late.

The primary finding about leisure is its contextual nature. Leisure is not leftover time, but a context for the expression of personal meaning and for social bonding. Leisure is not a set of secondary activities, but is a context in which things of importance may happen. It is connected, not segregated; meaningful more than peripheral. In the next section, we will use the intensive interviews to explore the content of that meaning further.

Leisure as Engagement

Leisure, as already outlined, is more than a collection of activities that fill leftover time. Underlying this study is the conceptualization of leisure as multidimensioned action in a variety of contexts. Leisure is distinguished from the economic roles of work and the intimacy and reproductive roles of family. On the other hand, any lines separating community, voluntary organization, and leisure roles are fuzzy at best. Therefore, this analysis divides the social world into the three main domains of work, family, and leisure. Leisure from this perspective includes such "serious" activity as religious participation, considerable political activity, and a lot of very disciplined effort put into acquiring skills that are not utilized directly in economic roles. Leisure, then, may be seen as a realm of engagement in which selves are invested and from which a variety of returns may be anticipated. While a dominant outcome is expected to be pleasure, such results as personal growth and development and wider and deeper relationships with others are also very much a part of leisure.

The aim here is not to define leisure with some set of clear parameters. Rather we will explore what leisure means and does in the lives of the 120 Peoria collaborators. In their stories, we found that leisure is—among other things—a social space, a resource, a dimension of life, a complement to other roles, and a realm of personal and social identity.

One of the questions guiding the study was whether leisure was a factor in later-life coping with change. When that question was asked directly, almost 80% of our sample said "Yes." The kind of help varied. The most common response (32%) was that leisure had been a context for maintaining or developing important relationships. Filling time or escape from problems was seen as leisure's primary contribution by 23%. Personal expression and development was reported by 12% with another 12% reporting both personal expression and social integration. Altogether 44% felt that leisure was a social context important to primary relationships. Yet, when these same persons were asked to identify any public program in which these contributions had been experienced, they almost all were unable to recall even one.

Leisure as a Social Space

Much of life is made up of obligations: employment, getting to and preparing for the job, taking care of a home, caring for children, responding to the special needs of significant others, and daily maintenance of ourselves and our possessions. In a rough way, leisure is identified as those areas of life that are relatively free from such obligation. Not that everything we need to do is ever completed, but we do carve out some time for activity that doesn't have to be done. Not only official vacations, but off-work time is supposed to be for more than getting ready to go back to work.

In this sense, leisure is a social space for action—socially sanctioned and even allotted some resources as a public good. It is also a social space for community—not without its expectations but devoted to expressing our bonds to the special others who are the immediate social contexts of our life journeys. There is, however limited our visions and self-defined possibilities, some element of doing what we want to do. A mechanic in a one-man repair shop was evaluating his life when he asked, "Isn't there more to life than work? When am I going to be able to do something that I really want to do?" With small children and an income directly tied to the time he puts in at his shop, where was the opportunity to do what he wanted for no reason other than he personally found it satisfying? In this sense, the expectation for leisure is seen as a right, not a frill.

For Nat (chapter 1) the venues of travel as well as the home are social spaces in which his family relationships are expressed. Alaska has been a place for the engrossing engagement of fishing. Now that he is retired he rebuilds old cars at home. But the "household of children," now three-generational, is central. Leisure and the family are especially tied together for other family-focused adults as well. Their leisure is centered around the family as they support the activities of their school-age children and grandchildren, allocate their time to joint activities, and see family relation-ships to be central to leisure's meanings. Even when launching their children, the family-focused tend to spend more time as couples, often in travel. Also, they often come to share leisure resources with their grand-children.

Eleanor (chapter 2) has had to cope with the death of two husbands, the second from war injuries. As a teacher, she was invested in her career. Leisure for her was primarily social. A woman's club, music groups, and church had been social settings where she made and retained the friend-ship of other women. The music group that had persisted from high school on is a remarkable example of how a leisure investment based on an action interest is at the same time a social space for significant community. For many others, religious organizations provide the same kind of continuity. Whatever else they may be, churches are voluntary organizations in which people of similar background and values may find long-term associations. They are a social space in which relationships of consistent caring and sharing are fostered.

Leisure as a Resource

As already indicated, 80% of the smaller sample said that leisure had been of some help in coping with change. Further, they were able to designate dimensions of that help:

1. Leisure is a social space for being with important others. For some experiencing broken relationships, it was a chance to form new rela-tionships. For Alice (chapter 2) her divorce was a turning point. At 49 she had full responsibility for herself and a small son. The two groups

that provided continuity have been her church and the women's barbershop chorus, the "Sweet Adelines." She isn't looking for another husband, but she wants and needs exchange and companionship with her peers. The factory wasn't the best place for friendship and now she has been laid off. Leisure for her is a domain in which to do things and be with other adults.

2. Leisure is a personal as well as a social resource. After Ethel's husband took off with another woman, she needed other people, to fill time and also to believe that she was a person of worth (chapter 3). She was urged to get out of the house and be more active. She joined a church group for the newly divorced, took up golf again, joined some clubs, did volunteer work, and travelled. She has had to rebuild a life style in which leisure is much more central to her schedule as well as a context for a redeveloped sense of self.

There is no guarantee that engagement with leisure will fill all voids and solve all problems. Amy (chapter 4) also uses leisure settings—plays, concerts, and other events—as social spaces to be with other adults. It helps, but is hardly a full substitute for the loss of intimacy caused by her divorce and estrangement from her son. Clara (chapter 4) has suffered a deterioration in her personal resources due to vision and health problems that have cut her off from some former leisure investments. Leisure has been about all she has had, but it isn't enough to compensate for the other domains in which she has experienced ego-shattering blows. Leisure is one resource for many, but not a panacea for all problems.

Leisure as a Dimension of Life

The fundamental reorientation of understanding leisure in this study is to see it as integrated with the rest of life rather than as a separate realm of activity. The balanced investors, especially those of high commitment, exemplify this well. They do not tend to divide life into separate domains, but are active and developing persons across times and places. This perspective is reinforced by an analysis of the mailed follow-up completed in the summer of 1984. In this survey, 217 completed instruments were received from the original 400 in the telephone sample. They completed a scale developed to assess motivational orientations (Steinkamp and Kelly, 1985). Statistical analysis of this Life Investment scale produced three dominant factors of motivation: challenge seeking, concern with recognition and reward, and family focus.

Scores on the Life Investment scale were correlated with a number of social factors, life satisfaction, and level of leisure activity. Challenge-seeking men and women and the retired had higher levels of leisure activity than those low in this motivational orientation. Further, family-focused women who had high levels of leisure activity were more satisfied with their lives than those less engaged in leisure. For retired men high in challenge-seeking orientations, however, leisure did not provide the same contribution to life satisfaction as for the sample as a whole. There is the likelihood that for such men leisure cannot adequately substitute for the feedback and recognition experienced in work. The family-focused, as expected, tended to be lowest in levels of leisure engagement.

Some of the interactions among leisure, motivation, and life-course roles appear to be rather complex. The point here is that leisure cannot be segregated either from other roles or from the ways in which we engage in those roles. Life may have varied and diverse settings for activity, but we are much the same persons from one to another. It is this continuity that comes through in so many of the collaborative interviews. Leisure is more a dimension of life than a separate realm of activity. In leisure we may attempt to work out many of the same agendas that we hold salient in other parts of life. Leisure, then, is a social space and a resource. It is, however, also a dimension of relative freedom to pursue our own aims in our own styles that is woven through the varied venues of engagement.

Another approach to this is found in the theme of religion. This is especially dramatic for some of the accepting adaptors. Whether or not they were associated with churches, they seemed to have absorbed the idea that God is the source of their life events. They define accepting the traumas and responsibilities of life as a religious duty. A few of the self-sufficient, on the other hand, had conventional relationships with churches, but seemed to believe that personal religion gave them strength to be independent. The older adults in both of these categories contrasted with the faithful members and many of the conventional balanced investors and family-focused for whom the church was more of a community of support. Religious participation, as one kind of voluntary organization engagement, becomes a venue of association with those who share values and cultural background. Those who incorporate religious ideologies in their coping styles, on the other hand, tend to be more accepting and passive than others in the sample.

Leisure as a Role Complement

In the 1950s a number of theorists suggested that leisure might be related to work as a "compensation" by providing escape or contrast to work conditions or as a "carryover" by extending work orientations and skills. Neither was found in research to be a dominant pattern. The issue of the relationship of leisure engagement to other roles remains important, however. More recently, the life-course model has been found to be more useful than the older work-leisure dichotomy (Rapoport and Rapoport, 1976). Through the life course, there are a number of work, family, leisure, and community roles that rise and fall in salience. These roles intersect in ways that are sometimes complementary and sometimes conflicting.

The developmental dilemmas of the life-course periods of preparation, establishment, and culmination are expressed in leisure domains as well as those of work and primary relationships (Kelly, 1983). During the teen years of preparation, leisure contexts may be most central to working out issues of social and sexual identity. For the older adults in our sample of 120, a number of themes recurred:

1. Those with children and sometimes grandchildren in school oriented considerable leisure time and effort to supporting school and extracurricular activities. Not only providing transportation, but attending, financing, and even coaching and teaching are common. Further, associations are developed with other parents that may endure after the children are launched. Vacations also tend to be family-oriented.

2. Efforts to take advantage of greater time and discretionary income resources after children are more or less "on their own" may lead to increased couple activity for those in intact marriages. Travel especially seems to provide an important context for such activity that may be partly aimed at expressing and strengthening the marital relationship.

3. Retirement leisure often has a sequence of engagements (Atchley, 1976). At first there may be an agenda of projects, trips, and other activities that require blocks of time. Once these are completed, however, it may be necessary to develop a more enduring set of engagements. The patterns vary. Balanced investors tend to continue the set of engagements that are already in place as well as utilize the blocks of time for travel. The family-focused are more likely to increase their participation in home enhancement and in primary group interaction. The self-sufficient often have one or two kinds of activity that are important. Faithful members become more involved in their extra-familial community. For the most part, continuity outweighs change. What is evident, however, is that the patterns are integrated into the life styles that are already under way. In fact, Don was not the only retiree who simply transferred his work-based self-definition to an achievement-oriented leisure activity (chapter 5). Leisure also became a more important setting for many whose work environment—such as a teachers' lounge—had been central to informal associations and friendships.

4. For those who have entered retirement complexes or nursing homes, leisure is generally confined largely to what can be done in that setting. Cards and conversation, TV and religious groups, and a variety of informal ways in which residents come together in dyads and groups

are the main contexts of association. Going out, perhaps to shop and for a meal, is often reserved for the time that family come to visit. The main dimension of meaning becomes the relationships and their expression rather than the kind of activities that are essayed.

Leisure, then, is tied to the major relationships and meanings of life. It is neither totally determined by other roles nor entirely separate. Rather, there is a shifting weave of relationships that reflects the role definitions, developmental orientations, resources, opportunities, and personal histories of each person making a life-course journey. Leisure is part of the weave, sometimes dominant and sometimes recessive, but always a part of the ever-changing whole.

Leisure as Identity

The "Who am I?" question is always important. The ways in which we define ourselves are central to how we direct our lives, respond to events, and allocate our resources. For most of the later-life adults who participated in this study, leisure was one integrated dimension of their life styles. For a few, some kind of sport or arts engagement was central to their personal and social identities. For most, leisure is one dimension of life that contributes to an identity that has several components.

The women balanced investors for whom membership in women's organizations was an important realm of meaning illustrate the latter pattern. Especially for those who had either no work career or family, such organizations provided opportunities for investment that yielded definitions of worth and significance. These women saw such activity as a positive contribution to the community as they worked consistently on projects that were perceived to be of value. They were women working with other women in organizations that provided a sense of purpose as well as ongoing associations with congenial and like-minded associates. In some cases, these associations were crucial when other domains of investment were lost or limited.

Leisure, then, is not either social or existential, a resource or time-filler, social space or a dimension, special or a role complement, personal or social identity, or any other dichotomy. Rather, it is "all of the above": inclusive rather than separate, multidimensioned rather than monothematic. Leisure is part of the life course, providing both continuity and novelty for those making the complex journey.

Opportunities and Programs

There is always the question of why so few older people participate in "Senior Citizen's" programs. We found a few who did, mostly as helpers rather than recipients of services. More common was Nat's comment that such places were for those who wanted to "sit around and exchange lies." Stereotypes of such programs are part of the inhibition. However, there are other factors:

1. Most adults have not established a pattern of active involvement in voluntary organizations. If they have found meaningful integration in one, it is usually a church, not a community organization.

2. Those who are most active are usually those with the most resources and opportunities. They continue or reorient old investments and have little time for joining something new. Their social patterns are more or less set before they retire. On the other hand, those with the fewest resources and the most inhibiting conditions often are just barely able to cope with the responsibilities and tasks they have already. They may need some help, but are unlikely to seek out a new engagement that will consume their already-meager resources of time, energy, transportation, and money.

3. Commitments to voluntary organizations are usually based in recognized commonalities of culture, interests, social status, and interests. Many older persons assume that they just wouldn't find "their own kind" at a public program that is open to anyone over some designated age.

4. Those with histories of activity in voluntary organizations tend to have been contributors. The image of senior programs is often one of having services "delivered" to them. That idea is inconsistent with their orientations toward joining anything. Further, most have had the experience that real community is a result of doing something together, not just being together.

There were exceptions. Eleanor (chapter 2) was very involved as a "helper" in a variety of organizations. She defines herself as a mother first, but as a young (early 60s) and active retiree she is out there helping older people rather than looking to receive help. Both her church and the Salvation Army provide organizational contexts for such activity. She is proactive and believes that "there is enough to do out there." She sees the problem as a failure of many to seek out opportunities.

It is always misleading to divide any part of the social world into two parts. The retirement-age people in our study do seem to represent two general styles, however. One set is engaged with other people and projects that have continuity with the past. Their lives are relatively full, if often somewhat prosaic and conventional. The other set is limited in resources and in something of a struggle to cope. They tend to be cut off from many sources of assistance outside their immediate communities. Those who are most likely to respond to new opportunities for older persons either do not have fairly full lives or need help in order to participate. Further, since people join new groups largely through the mediation of others whom they know, the small participation base of most senior programs is self-limiting.

The critical question is how those who need fuller engagement and community can be drawn into programs that are oriented toward meeting such needs. Here all we offer is some insight for identifying such persons and understanding why the number is limited.

Summary

Is leisure a resource for coping with later-life change? The answer may be affirmative, but a little less simple than might have been expected. Leisure is not a filler of gaps as much as a context for action and interaction that is integrated with the life-course sequence of roles and resources. It is a factor in coping, especially for those who have made consistent investment in self-developing and community-building engagement. On the other hand, leisure pulled into a life style to substitute for other dimensions is not likely to fill an otherwise empty or emptied life. The exception to this seems to be for relatively active persons who have had a major domain of investment—family or work—withdrawn. They may devote more attention to leisure engagements, usually those with which they are already involved. Leisure may then offer possibilities of meaningful action and community. And for some in the process of a major life transition, leisure may be a life space that does fill some voids, at least until significant investments are renewed.

References

Atchley, Robert H. 1976. *The Sociology of Retirement.* Cambridge, MA: Schenkman.
Gordon, Chad, C. Gaitz, and J. Scott. 1976. "Personal Expressivity across the Life Cycle." In *Handbook of Aging and the Social Sciences,* R. Binstock and E. Shanas, eds. New York: Van Nostrand Reinhold.
Havighurst, Robert. 1957. "The Leisure Activities of the Middle Aged." *American Journal of Sociology* 63:152–162.
Kelly, John R. 1978. "Situational and Social Factors in Leisure Decisions." *Pacific Sociological Review* 21:313–333.
———. 1982. *Leisure.* Englewood Cliffs, NJ: Prentice-Hall.
———. 1983. *Leisure Identities and Interactions.* London and Boston: Allen and Unwin.
———. 1987. *Freedom To Be: A New Sociology of Leisure.* New York: Macmillan.
Kelly, John R., Marjorie Steinkamp, and Janice R. Kelly. 1986. "Later Life Leisure: How They Play in Peoria." *The Gerontologist* 26:531–537.
———. 1987. "Later Life Satisfaction: Does Leisure Contribute?" *Leisure Sciences* 10:1.

Kleiber, Douglas A. 1985. "Motivational Reorientation in Adulthood and the Resource of Leisure." In *Motivation and Adulthood,* D. Kleiber and M. Maehr, eds. Greenwich, CT: JAI Press.

Lemon, B.W., V. Bengtson, and J. Peterson. 1972. "An Exploration of the Activity Theory of Aging: Activity Types and Life Satisfaction among In-movers to a Retirement Community." *Journal of Gerontology* 27:511–523.

Longino, C.F., and C. Kart. 1982. "Explicating Activity Theory: A Formal Replication." *Journal of Gerontology* 37:713–722.

McGuire, Francis A., D. Dottavio, and J. O'Leary. 1986. "Constraints to Participation in Outdoor Recreation across the Life Span: A Nationwide Study." *The Gerontologist* 26:538–544.

Neugarten, Berniece L., ed. 1968. *Middle Age and Aging.* Chicago: University of Chicago Press.

Neugarten, B.L., R. Havighurst, and S. Tobin. 1961. "The Measurement of Life Satisfaction." *Journal of Gerontology* 16:134–143.

Okun, M., W. Stock, M. Haring, and R. Witter. 1984. "The Social Activity/Well-Being Relation." *Research on Aging* 6:45–65.

Palmore, Erdman. 1979. "Predictors of Successful Aging." *The Gerontologist* 19:427–431.

Peppers, L. 1977. "Patterns of Leisure and Adjustment to Retirement." *The Gerontologist* 16:441–446.

Rapoport, Rhona, and R.N. Rapoport. 1976. *Leisure and the Family Life Cycle.* London: Routledge and Kegan Paul.

Roberts, Kenneth. 1978. *Contemporary Society and the Growth of Leisure.* London: Longmans.

Steinkamp, Marjorie, and J. Kelly. 1985. "Relationships among Motivational Orientations, Level of Leisure Activity, and Life Satisfaction among Older Men and Women." *Journal of Psychology* 119:509–520.

8
Social Integration: Helping and Sharing

One of the critical issues in social gerontology is that of "caregiving." A number of subissues have emerged as more and more attention is given to problems associated with increased longevity that is often accompanied by dependence on others.

One issue, of course, is who does the caretaking. Although the risk of institutionalization increases with age, at any one time only about 5% of adults over age 65 are being cared for in intermediate or full-care institutions. Even though the myth of the idyllic three-generational household that cared for and honored the frail elderly has been largely laid aside (Kent, 1965), the burden of caretaking does seem to fall on family and especially adult children. Brody (1985) has carried out a series of studies that confirm both the primacy of family caregiving and common stresses on the responsible family members. The norm of parent care has even been proposed as a common life-course period that ought to be anticipated rather than come as a surprise. Brody has argued that parent care falls primarily on women, that such care may be a repeated rather than one-time event, that caretaking may interfere with work careers and roles, and that conflicting expectations produce stress. Further, there is a reduction in "total" care from "the old days" that may produce feelings of inadequacy and even guilt among the adult children.

A related issue is that of how caregivers define their roles and how they feel about those being helped. Some research has found that there seems to be a frequent reduction in affection toward those being helped, especially as the conflicts and demands increase (Jarrett, 1985). The motivational orientation often shifts from affection and "love" to duty and responsibility. In this shift, the adult caregiver may experience inner tension between resentment at the demands and feeling guilty about the diminution of affection.

The traditional questions, therefore, revolve around who helps the frail elderly and how they feel about it. Most research has concentrated on those periods of maximum impact as older parents, spouses, or other family members become increasingly dependent. The causes may be the age-indexed loss of independence related to the synergy of health changes or due to a particular traumatic syndrome such as Alzheimer's disease. While family members have been found to be the usual primary support providers, how friends and neighbors supplement or substitute for family care and the place of community programs are also under study (Shanas, 1979; Brody, 1985). Much remains to be learned about just how informal networks of social interaction and support operate and are complemented by formal programs (Ward, 1985).

This chapter is not intended as a full review or analysis of the issues of social integration and support in later life. Rather, a single insight from the Peoria study is offered as a supplement to more inclusive research agendas. Focus is on a single issue: how the career of interaction with family and friends makes the relationships more complex than the "helper" or "caretaker" image suggests.

In any research, we are likely to find at least some suggestion of what we are looking for. After all, any research design limits the world under investigation, focuses on particular dimensions of that delimited world, and attempts to measure those selected elements. When research is designed to examine common dimensions of helping such as financial, transportation, logistical, health, and emotional support, then measures of their direction and magnitude are central to the design. On the other hand, when the focus is on contexts of interaction, then a broader picture of relationships is likely to be found.

The Peoria Study: Who Helped?

In our study, we addressed the issue of helping from a different direction. First, we identified major changes through the later-life course. Second, we asked who had been of help in coping with those changes. Third, we attempted to get a fuller view of the contexts of those relationships. As outlined in the previous chapter, we thought it likely that leisure contexts of various kinds played some part in relationships with significant helpers. It seemed possible that leisure might make its primary contribution to the lives of older adults as a context for the development and expression of significant relationships. That is, leisure would be one aspect of social integration with family and friends.

Our surprise was that leisure activity was found to be more than just a social context. Rather, there is an independent contribution from nonwork engagements that is integrated with the sequence of roles and orientations of the later-life course. This finding, however, did not close the question of the relationship of leisure to social integration.

Our answer to the first question: "Who helped?" was no different from the results of previous research. The likelihoods are obvious: we are most likely to receive assistance from those who are close and available, those who care and for whom we care, and those with the resources to give help. Just who those persons are varies through the life course and with the particular circumstances:

1. For those in an intact and communicative marriage, the first provider of logistical and emotional support is usually the spouse. The spouse is also the one with whom our collaborators were most likely to talk things over.

2. For widowed parents, their adult children, especially if nearby, were most likely to provide advice, emotional support, and other kinds of needed help at times of crisis and change.

3. Many older informants also referred to one or more sisters, brothers, or other extended family as being of crucial help. This help, however, was no more common than references to a particular friend. Such intimate friends, especially for women, often are experiencing similar changes. They are "peers" in their histories and can share in the impacts and responses to transitions and traumas.

4. Such peer friends were also significant for older adults who lacked family relationships due to distance, dissolution of relationships, or never being married.

5. Less commonly mentioned were professionals. When professional helpers were mentioned it was usually in relation to a specific trauma. Further, the advice was more often technical rather than general. Those mentioned as giving such help were, in order of frequency: clergy, doctors, lawyers, and counselors. For some recovered alcoholics, professional counseling had been of assistance.

6. There were also the self-sufficients who were mostly likely to respond "no one" when asked who helped. As already indicated, some are cut off from resources, unusually self-reliant, or both.

7. If any voluntary organization had been of assistance, it was almost always the church for persons who had prior social integration within some religious community.

As suggested, then, on this question there were no real surprises. Our findings are completely consistent with other research on the same question. Who helps? Those who are there and with whom there is a history of bonding.

A Different Question

There is a somewhat different question, however. Rather than simply identifying the helpers, we wanted to know more about the "non-helping" dimensions of those relationships. Especially with the evidence of a possible loss of affection when caretaking becomes prolonged and burdensome, are there other aspects of these relationships that might mitigate resentment and ameliorate the burden?

Analysis of the stories of change, coping, and resources begins with what is reported. Our summary is simple: for the most part, "helpers" are also "sharers." Those to whom our collaborators turned for all kinds of support were those with whom they shared other dimensions of their lives. Helping was one theme of multidimensioned relationships and usually not the dominant one.

As expected, this combining of expressive and instrumental dimensions in relationships is most evident among the family-focused. There are many instances of financial and logistical support: taking a granddaughter to radiation therapy, buying household goods for parents with below-subsistance income, and caring for children during times of special need or just to give some relief. The main issue, however, is emotional support. It is crucial that particular family members are sure to be there, to be available when needed. Throughout the changes in work, family, residence, health, or economic circumstances, it was spouse, children, or siblings who were most likely to "be there" to help. The nature of the help was manifold: counsel, listening, talking it over, advice, and sometimes economic assistance.

When children are in trouble, the main source of support is, if available, the spouse. When husbands leave, it is adult children or a brother or sister. When serious surgery is impending, a daughter crosses the country to be there. When a widow needs someone to talk to, it is most likely to be a daughter or a close friend who is also a widow. When an older woman in an intermediate-care facility needs to get out and do some shopping, her granchildren share the responsibility.

The point is that these are the same people who have shared significant parts of a life history. They are the same ones who have been through other changes together. They have shared life's celebrations as well as troubles, vacation trips as well as times of loss and mourning, games as well as tasks. They have driven to ball games and concerts, gathered around the Christmas tree, and run from the rain or mosquitoes together at the summer picnic. They may be helpers in a particular time, but they have been primary "sharers" more often. Even for those households that have experienced continual poverty, there has been the sharing of all the times of joy as well as of strain and deprivation.

Despite the common divisions of life into domains such as work, leisure, family, school, church, and polity, life as lived tends to be much more of an integrated whole. This does not mean that commuting to a workplace that children have never seen is not a *dis*integrating condition for many households. Nor do we have all the same companions in every social world. Nevertheless, our bonding with those who form our primary groups of family and friends usually crosses the analytical boundaries.

Nat is an example of one who centers his life in his family ties even though he has had significant work and leisure investments. Eva (chapter 3) cannot separate interaction with her husband and sons in their contracting business from the history of nurturing children, grandchildren, and foster children. Life centers around those relationships of sharing and mutual activity with multiple dimensions often woven together in a single event or period. Now that the business is in trouble, it is a family problem that they are trying to work out together. Over and over, we heard interpretations of life in which central meanings and satisfaction were indissolubly intertwined with a full range of life events that had been shared.

Trauma may even intensify that sense of bonding. It did so for Ray who has stopped drinking and who now is a provider of support and advice for others in the extended family (chapter 3). For a functionally illiterate factory worker who had been an alcoholic up to the age of 48, that is a remarkable recovery of sharing.

Family is not the only source of such bonding. Bridget (chapter 4) has become a faithful member in her adult years and has not allowed residence in a care facility to impede such meaningful relationships. From a family so poor that she had to leave school in eighth grade to go to work, she has come to define herself as a helper through the strength that she has received from a Catholic renewal movement and nondenominational groups and broadcasts. In her case, however, the relationships are more in a group mode than a set of one-to-one ties.

What is provided in such significant sharing relationships? When necessary and possible, there have been instances of logistical and financial help. Money has been given or loaned. Transportation has been provided. There have also been periods in which advice has been needed about legal, financial, or other practical matters. Central, however, has been the stable relationship of communication and trust. Most important has been the confidence that the other can be relied on not to pull away. Especially when there has been instability or betrayal on the part of a spouse or significant other, those who can be relied on become especially important to coping. As good times have often been shared through the life course, now the losses and hurts can be shared as well. "Helping" connotes a one-way flow of giving of various kinds. "Sharing" suggests that two or more people are going through the changes together.

Social Integration Reanalyzed

A central question underlying the design of the Peoria study was whether the main contribution of leisure to later-life coping was in providing contexts for social integration. In other words, was it consistent supportive interaction with significant others that was crucial to coping with change? When older adults had the prerequisites of adequate health and financial resources, was the next important factor social integration? If so, then leisure would contribute indirectly rather than directly. As reported in the previous chapter, leisure was found to make a major and independent contribution to later life satisfaction. On the other hand, primary relationships were also found to provide the main social support in times of change. Can these two findings be brought into some perspective?

In the telephone survey of 400 adults, social integration was measured by frequency of interaction with family and friends. This quantitative social integration score was employed in the first round of analysis to examine the question of coping with change. Then we examined leisure activities and orientations to see if they were strongly biased toward interaction with significant others.

The findings displayed in figure 8–1 were not as clear as anticipated:

1. Such regular interaction with family and friends was relatively stable for men and women with two exceptions. Women most likely to still have children at home were much less likely to interact regularly with friends and extended family. More important, there was a much lower level of interaction for those age 75 and above.

2. There was also a strong negative relationship between education level and social integration. This was found in the intensive interviews to reflect the lower education levels of the family-focused who were less involved outside the family and the limited social resource histories of accepting adaptors.

3. Social integration, on the other hand, was lower for the never married, but not for the divorced or widowed.

4. There was a strong correlation between leisure activity level and frequency of social interaction. This expected finding led to further analysis decomposing the relationship.

The problem at this point was that the inclusion of family and social activities in the list of types of leisure was confounded with the quantitative measure of social integration. It was inevitable that social integration with both family and friends would be strongly correlated with levels of leisure activity since each measure contained items that were close to being duplicates. Even so, there were some inconsistencies. One was that social integration with friends had a stronger association with life satisfaction for men (Gamma = .295) than for women (Gamma = .046). Further, there was no relationship found between frequency of interaction with family and life

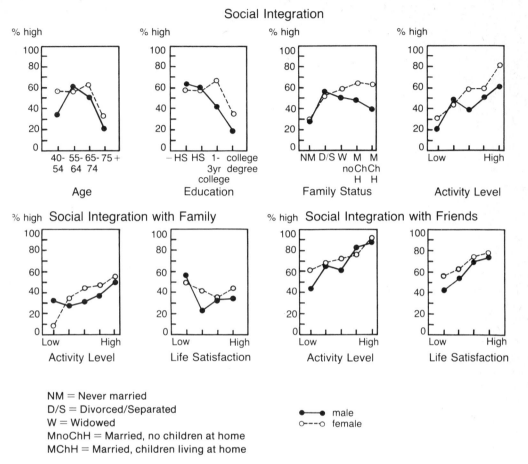

Figure 8–1. Percentages with High Levels of Social Integration

satisfaction. Rather, along with resources, the primary factor was leisure engagement.

The next step was to examine these relationships by age to see if they hold for all 40-and-over categories. Employing discriminant function analysis that identifies factors distinguishing preselected groups, age differences were found. First, for those 75 and over, being married or not becomes the primary factor in social integration followed by level of activity. Second, for all except those between the ages of 55 and 64, family activities are the primary basis of social integration as measured by frequency of interaction. Again, the overlap between family and social kinds of leisure and the integration measure made this finding less than startling.

Fortunately, a second set of measures was included in the design. "Subjective integration" was measured by twelve items that asked about loneliness, a sense of belonging, being appreciated by family and friends, having enough friends, and relating to others (Steinkamp and Kelly, unpublished paper). These items were combined into a scale with a possible maximum score of 48 and found to have a mean of 16.7 and a standard deviation of 4.5. Using a multiple regression model of analysis, demographic variables were included with subjective integration, frequency of interaction with family and friends, and leisure activity level. Subjective life satisfaction was the dependent variable. The salient findings are as follows:

1. Problems and limiting life conditions such as health and finances were negatively related to satisfaction accounting for 12% of the variance. These subjective measures of deficits refer to the personal and social resources that have been found to be "prerequisites" of later-life coping.

2. Only for males over 65 did the frequency of interaction correlate significantly with subjective well-being. Older men seem to define the quality of their relationships more in terms of actual interaction than do women or preretirement men.

3. When the subjective measure of social integration was added to the equation, it added significantly to the variance of life satisfaction with Beta coefficients of .43 for men 65 and over, .25 for women under 65, and .20 for women 65 and over. The perceived quality of relationships was significant for all women and for retirement-age men.

4. Further, leisure activity level does not contribute significantly to perceived life satisfaction for either men or women over 65 in this analysis. When the older-age segment is analyzed separately, the original hypothesis seems to be supported. Leisure is most important as a context for those significant "sharing" relationships that support and sustain coping with the changes associated with retirement and the final period of life.

5. Also, what is important, especially for women, is the quality rather than quantity of relationships. Although this is not surprising since the correlation is between two evaluations or perceptions rather than between a set of conditions and perceptions, it does suggest several likelihoods consistent with the analyses of the cases:

    a. There is a social constriction of life in later years. This shrinking of geographical and social circles makes those primary relationships that endure of overriding importance.

    b. Family and friends who are of such significance are still those with whom many dimensions of life, including leisure, are shared.

c. It is the quality rather than quantity of social relationships that is crucial to later-life coping and satisfaction.

d. Leisure, increasingly social, familial, and home-based through the final part of the life course, more and more reflects those significant relationships rather than the resources and engagements that take adults into different environments and engagements. The function of leisure, then, seems to shift somewhat for those experiencing that constriction of environments and investments.

Even though this research is not longitudinal, the findings of the cross-sectional analysis are consistent with the stories of those who were looking back in the collaborative interviews.

Accounts of Social Integration

Life Course Differences

First, social integration has somewhat different meanings for those in different periods of the life course. The Peoria adults who still had children at home usually centered at least a portion of their social ties around their support and activities. A university professor (chapter 2) was very engaged in his work and in professional associations—too engaged, in his own view. His social life included a major component of associations and interactions with the parents of his children's peers. They participated together in a variety of support activities, attended events, and shared those common experiences. He is a balanced investor who believes that he is currently over-invested and anticipates some relief as the children are launched.

At the other extreme, those who are now caretakers for parents or spouses who require considerable attention may find their social circles quite limited. They cannot get too far away or commit extended periods of time to any other line of action. Like those who are bound to their residence by infirmities, such caretakers are experiencing social constriction even when their own capabilities are unimpaired.

The situation of retired men in our sample also reflects a significant change in their life conditions. For them, regular interaction with friends is more important to life satisfaction than for any others in the study. Retired men seem to find it necessary to replace workplace associations with other interactions outside the family. Some do this through voluntary associations, some in neighborhood and friendship activity, and some widowers by eating meals regularly in a restaurant that has become a meeting place. Since Peoria has no real equivalent of the British "local" pub, accessible locales for informal gathering are more difficult to find.

Contexts for Interaction

The contexts in which social integration is expressed and developed also change through the life course. For Ellen, the retirement center where she lives is the usual site for interaction with other residents as well as with her sons when they visit (chapter 3). Her account of changes in social environments is typical although she was widowed at age 41. While her boys were in school, she was active in PTA and other child-oriented organizations. As they became more involved in their own lives, she took up other volunteer work and music. Now her health keeps her tied to the home, and she has only that context remaining.

Jim, on the other hand, is 30 years younger at 51, but is beset with economic insecurity. Having launched his children and fully ready to be a good grandfather, his layoff has caused him to limit his engagements to ones that are relatively cost-free. His history of drinking and participation in very active "masculine" activities turned in toward the family when he dealt with his alcoholism. Now his intermittent employment has brought another change to his patterns of activity. Both transitions and traumas have their impacts on the contexts of social interaction. This year Jim has no plans for a Wyoming hunting trip, formerly the high point of his year.

Alice is a balanced investor who had to reconstruct her life after a divorce (chapter 2). She meets friends in church, interacts with other Boy Scout parents, and is a regular in the women's barbershop singing group. When her job folded, she went back to school for retraining. In all these settings, she has regular interaction with friends. Note that she is one of many who is divorced and no longer has the previous "couple" set of associations.

The locales of interaction shift through the life course and intersect with the major roles of the period. Sometimes adults have to seek out times and places to be with peers. For the most part, however, those contexts are a natural part of the social worlds of individuals who have a role set appropriate to their work, family, and community roles. Interaction and integration are consequences of responding to the expectations, responsibilities, and opportunities of that period of life. When a trauma disrupts those contexts, however, remedial action may be required to fill the social voids. In the final years characterized by increasing fragility, the social contexts are pulled into a tighter and tighter circle and reliance on family becomes crucial for most.

Subjective Integration and Women

Quite a number of the women in our study repeatedly referred to a special friend. Most often that friend was another woman of about the same age who was in a parallel life situation. For widows, the friend was usually also widowed. Sometimes the friendships dated back to school, sometimes to parenting associations, and sometimes to neighborhood interaction. Close friends were often "old friends," but not always.

Some would argue that women are better prepared for such close friendships than men, that the intimacy of trust and open communication goes back as far as the times of having a teen "best friend." Further, it may be that males have lived in a competitive and structured social world that facilitates more instrumental and limited relationships. Mary's friend Helen is crucial to her coping with her stormy marriages and two divorces (chapter 1). They talk almost every evening as well as participate in the dance group together. Helen shares the problems of adjusting to divorce, rebuilding a life, and joining a church group as well as dancing. Both are in their 60s and are determined to have full lives with plenty of interaction with others. Their communication now has its own special place in their lives, but has certainly been facilitated by the opportunities for mutual activity.

Again, it is the quality rather than the quantity of social relationships that contributes to the life satisfaction of women at any age. Friendships may not have the special bonds of kinship (Rubin, 1985), but may have considerable depth and continuity. Research that defines social integration as either the number and frequency of informal associations or the range of formal organizational memberships may be off target. It is the quality of communication and sharing with available significant others that really makes the difference.

We should not, however, assume that all women are destined for such intimacy. Self-sufficients have coping styles characterized more by independence than intimacy. Marian (chapter 5) was divorced once and widowed in her second marriage. Moving often from one community to another, she is sure that she has to live for herself because there is no one to do it for her. She keeps busy, relies primarily on herself, and had to find new associations because she was widowed at a younger age than most of her friends. She does have a close friend with whom she eats out at least twice a week. She has had to reconstruct her social network so often that she seems reluctant to be too dependent on anyone. She does, however, seek contexts for communication and sharing.

Marian is somewhere between Mary and Winnie on the intimacy or special relationship continuum. Winnie (chapter 5) had been driven to exhaustion by the requirements to provide for her children when her husband's health failed. She has only very occasional exchanges with her closest woman friend, as infrequently as once a month. She also is able to be with her grown children some. For the most part, however, she finds her strength in the times that she can manage to be alone.

We would not want to stereotype adult women as always having or requiring the support of at least one intimate friend. Women can be independent, too, especially when they have had to learn to be. Nevertheless, the theme of sharing in a reciprocity with dimensions of information, counsel, emotional support, empathy, and trust is common enough to be given special attention for adult women.

Sharing through the Later-Life Course

What is social integration? And, who are those who give support and help in the later-life course? The answer to the second question seems clear: those with whom we share our lives. And the answer to the first question is related: social integration is the sharing.

This sharing has one "normal" sequence for parents in intact marriages. Most often that sharing revolves around the sequential tasks of parenting for the couple until they reach that "golden pond" of grandparenting in which they have satisfactions of developmental interaction with fewer obligations. There is, of course, considerable providing, supporting, guiding, and helping all along the way. Grandparents provide more than occasional companionship in most cases. As with parenting, the meanings and satisfactions are tied to being needed as well as being enjoyed. The relationships that comprise social integration tend to be multidimensional rather than segmental.

"Sharing" describes many of the one-to-one relationships of intimacy and support as well as the group relationships of family or household. Intimacy in the sense of openness, depth and breadth of communication, trust, and continuity is at the center of such sharing. From a group rather than dyadic perspective, the key term may be "community." Community connotes a sharing of central life interests, social contexts, and roles. There is a continuity to community that offers reliable access through life course changes. While the family is the most common such community, there are others: church, neighborhood, or voluntary organizations.

Balanced investors and faithful members are those most often involved in such communities other than the family. They have most often made commitments to such communities that give them alternative sources of support and sharing when life courses have turning points or zigzags. Even those who are relatively conventional can turn to such social contexts when they have lost other sources of support.

The critical issues in later life, then, seem to be those of constricted social circles and the consequent loss of community. Is there an almost inevitable narrowing down to sharing with just a few, usually family and those in the immediate living situation? If we live long enough, do we almost always lose those wider sets of relationships that have provided opportunities for sharing in earlier periods? And, if that process is general and even inevitable, then is there anything that can be done to mitigate its effects? This brings us back to the issue of caretakers.

If we need reliable relationships to cope with change and if such relationships are reduced in scope in the final period of life, then the answer may be simple. Those related to others who have shared their lives and who take the responsibility of support just have to recognize that such support is a part of the life course. Those who lack the support of such caring others will have to be provided substitutes in whatever is the most viable living context for their capabilities.

Or, is there the possibility of another alternative? Are there ways in which community can be renewed or reconstructed? If the clue is that support most often comes from those who have shared many dimensions of life, then contexts for such sharing might be developed. Are there mutual activities that are more than time-filling and possible for older people who are limited and relatively isolated? Can they be brought together to share activity that they define as significant? One hint may be found in the few from our sample involved in programs for "senior citizens." They were more likely to be helpers than recipients.

References

Brody, Elaine M. 1985. "Parent Care as a Normative Family Stress." *The Gerontologist* 25:19–29.

Jarrett, William H. 1985. "Caregiving within Kinship Systems: Is Affection Really Necessary?" *The Gerontologist* 25:5–10.

Kent, Donald P. 1965. "Aging—Fact and Fancy." *The Gerontologist* 5.2.

Rubin, Lillian. 1985. *Just Friends.* New York: Basic Books.

Shanas, Ethel. 1979. "The Family as Social Support System in Old Age." *The Gerontologist* 19:169–174.

Steinkamp, Marjorie, and J. Kelly. 1985. "Social Integration, Leisure Activity, and Life Satisfaction in Older Adults." Unpublished paper.

Ward, Russell A. 1985. "Informal Networks and Well-Being in Later Life: A Research Agenda." *The Gerontologist* 25:55–61.

9
The Clear Costs
of Social Class

A decade and a half ago, Richard Sennett wrote an influential analysis of *The Hidden Injuries of Class* (Sennett and Cobb, 1973). The book develops the argument that economic measures of social stratification are inadequate. Even analyses of the institutional ramifications of differences in resources and power are only the beginning. Rather, urban industrial workers perceive threats to the fundamental context of their lives that are out of their control. In a series of 150 interviews in Boston, Sennett and Cobb probed how workers defined their lives and how they felt about that criterion of social class, their "life chances."

Sennett wrote of several dimensions of injury that underlay such indices as income, occupational status and mobility, and levels of education. What are the consequences of a lack of ability to determine the course of one's own life, of being channelled into circumstances in which there are few options for self-creating action? Within the stratified social system, some are led from their social origins to accept symbols of inability, the loss of dignity and a sense of accomplishment when sacrifice for others has been betrayed, and having to accept a social definition of always being replaceable. The "hidden injuries" that Sennett identifies are the limited and defensive self-definitions that are fostered by these conditions.

Not the details but the general thrust of that argument came to mind over and over while the collaborative interviews were listened to and analyzed. There were, of course, the pathetic stories of lives that had been launched with acute limitations and which now were in conditions of high demand and few resources. These stories were only partly mitigated by Mary and others who had managed to overcome such limitations to build a satisfying life. But there was something more: a sense that no list of variables or least squares analysis could quite portray how those limitations had shaped inner as well as outer lives. What were the "hidden injuries" that were far more profound than any indices of status or resources could suggest?

When social class is identified as the differential "life chances" or set of opportunities based on economic position, then there is no question that we live in a society that has produced and reproduced vast disparities. From their family of orientation, some have a wide range of developmental, educational, and social opportunities. "Money is no object" in providing them with preparation and opportunity. Others are raised in families that combine more limited resources with values that give priority to allocating those resources toward enhancing the life chances of their children. A few in our Peoria sample, however, had left school after a few years because there wasn't enough household income to feed and clothe everyone. Many others had moved from public school directly into a set of responsibilities that compounded through the life course into an "iron cage" (Weber, 1930) with few if any alternatives evident. Reflection on those stories yielded the conviction that the "injuries," the composite life circumstances, were not "hidden" but quite manifest and clear.

Manifest Injuries

A life-course perspective on social class is somewhat different from a one-time identification based on placement in the economic system and consequent social power and resources. Studies of mobility take measures of family origin and then identify an adult time as the arrival at class designation (Bendix and Lipset, 1966). Considerable research has demonstrated that the social conditions of the family or origin are the greatest single influence on arrival class. Such diachronic analysis is useful, but does not take account of what has occurred in between. More recent longitudinal analysis has been able to catalog some intermediary events and their effects (Sewell and Hauser, 1975).

A life-course analysis presupposes that the effects of class are cumulative. Unless some event or action wrenches an individual out of a class-based trajectory, every cost and limitation will compound to solidify life chances. The "snowballing" metaphor might be employed if it could include rolling on bare and rocky ground. The life that begins with few opportunities will most often continue forward in social and economic environments in which there are relatively few opportunities to pick up new resources. The stories of many of our collaborators illustrate how those who begin with resources are more likely to add others along the way.

Resource Limitations

The most manifest cost of social class is in the vast differences in institutional resources that are perpetuated through the life course. To take a "success" as our first example, there is the story of Mary (chapter 1) who has managed to become a relatively satisfied balanced investor. She was clearly of low social class for most of her life—she did laundry and sewing for others during her two marriages to troubled and destructive men and had completed only ten years of school. Raised during the Depression as one of ten children, she began employment at age 16, graduated into marriage with an emotionally unstable man followed by divorce and then 15 years married to an alcoholic. What she had going for her was considerable native ability and a determination that she would make it for herself and her children no matter what. That she now is respected in her office job and is invested in several groups and activities is evidence that no set of circumstances can completely determine just how a person will create her own life within and out of those conditions. Nevertheless, Mary's inner strength— perhaps due to a family of origin that was not poor in the quality of their relationships—had to be utilized to overcome a history that left her with little else except her children at age 45.

Several other cases demonstrate how class origins limit the gathering of resources through the life course. Leaving school early, or even being illiterate, restricted many of our Peoria adults to sequences of menial, insecure, and low-paid jobs in which they could always be replaced by someone else. Both the women who cleaned houses for others and the men who were looking for odd jobs after being laid off as factory hands lacked later-life resources because they had not had opportunities to develop their abilities when young. The point is that resources are cumulative, or not. They cannot be reduced to a set of variables that are orthogonal and discrete.

Life on the Margins

The social system works best for those who move through its institutional roles accepting the on-time opportunities and statuses that accrue in the "normal" course of events. Mary was an exceptional balanced investor in transcending her history of limitations. Most had been able to gain from the family, school, and community resources directed at "mainstream" children, youth, and adults. They were able to invest themselves in multiple roles and engagements because they had been prepared to recognize and enter the doorways to such investment. They had gained the resources to pass over the thresholds that progressively denied access to others.

Just as building resources is cumulative for those within the system, so deprivation is progressively depleting for those on the margins. For Francis (chapter 6) "buying all those shoes" symbolized just how close she had been to not making it for years. Raised in a black family with 13 brothers, she had been married and divorced after six years. She had six children to support and worked for 23 years as a postal clerk despite only nine years of public school. Her problems always had a financial core. She is an accepting adaptor who never really had much time to reflect on her life conditions. She was always too involved in doing what had to be done. Her life was continually on the margins of financial disaster and of personal exhaustion. She really never had the resources to become deeply invested in anything other than keeping her family afloat. As a consequence, now at age 72, she receives and makes family visits, tends her small apartment, and gets through the day.

Investment, after all, presupposes some discretionary resources. There is at least some supra-marginal amount of time, energy, and money. For those who have always been on the margins without much perceived discretion, life is a day-to-day affair. It is accepting realities, living with limits, and getting through the day and maybe the week.

Opportunity Structures

From an individualistic point of view, we may view opportunities as items on a supermarket counter. We walk along and reach out to pick off those that attract us. We may recognize that some counters are more varied than others and that some shoppers can't afford everything. The market metaphor, however, is often implicitly employed in discussions of choices and possibilities.

From a more sociological perspective, the regularities of what is available are part of the social system. Our supermarket becomes a nightmare for those who cannot afford most of the offerings. And there are others who live too far away or who are not allowed inside at all. There are, then, structures of opportunity. In a stratified society, the market metaphor breaks down in several ways. First, some can't even get close enough to look through the window. Second, others are there but are outside the resource system that provides exchange values for those opportunity items. Third, and most important, for those on the margins of the system, opportunities taken for granted by mainstream participants are not even part of their real world. Life isn't choice: it is coping. And those who sail by hardly see those just barely keeping their heads above water.

What is the appropriate metaphor of life chances for the women who made it by cleaning other people's homes? For Florence (chapter 6), cleaning homes was a step up from cleaning at a nursing home and motel. Her mentally ill husband is at home. Bills from her own surgery are still coming in to add to her husband's medication cost. She has no pension ahead, no health plan, and no chance of things getting better. There is Elizabeth (chapter 6, p. 1) who couldn't even get her garden in last year. Did these women make some errors in judgment for which they can be held responsible? They are moral, responsible, hard-working, honest, and would even go to church if they had the time and transportation.

Their marginality is not a matter of attitude or aptitude. Their life journeys have been made in a social system that never allowed them onto the freeway. With so much rejoicing over the almost vanished correlation between age and poverty, we need to recognize that there are still those who never made it into the reward system at all. They never got to the doorway, much less over the threshold. And note something else, these marginal and aging persons are not getting any special attention and help from the service agencies of their community. Unlike their more privileged neighbors, they often don't even know whom to call for help.

Social Class as Life Chances

Out of school early, into the work force at minimum wage, coping with family responsibilities and often alone, facing illness without insurance, and entering old age without any resources beyond next week: these are the life chances of a few of our collaborators. How many? It depends on how we measure life chances. Also, our small sample makes percentages only rough indicators of anything. However, we had at least 20 with histories of cumulative deprivation. That gives us between 15 and 20%, just about the national poverty figure according to cost-adjusted calculations. Again, remember that most of these persons are not on welfare and have been economically self-sufficient most of their lives.

A history of deprivation and problems does not always lead to passive acceptance and certainly not to despair. One family-focused woman in her 60s (chapter 3) has had a life filled with family and friends. She is close to her husband and enjoys four grandchildren. That's the good part. The other side is that she had spent 37 years in a factory, has a heart condition and diabetes, and has no real interests outside her immediate circle. Having left school early to go to work, her life has always been a round of work and family. It has worked for her because her family in intact and close. Her marriage provides communication and companionship, not universal for women in her situation (Rubin, 1976). Her life is a "success" in terms of expressed satisfaction. Yet, it is also very limited in scope. Think of all those hours on the factory floor: 37 years times 40 hours a week and ended not by choice but by a heart attack. She went through life just above the margins and one event away from having to cope with drastically altered circumstances.

Of course, there are always a few like Alma (chapter 2) out there who just blast right through class-based limitations with incredible drive and direction. Granted her investments in racial justice and in improvements in the circumstances of black people in Peoria have been supported by her husband, ten children, and others. She somehow "did it all" and more with minimal social resources. In a different way, however, Alma's history is also one of cumulative competencies, identities, and resources. For her the snowballing worked, but she provided most of the momentum herself.

We would never argue that there is some sort of social determinism at work in our society that makes certain outcomes inevitable. Alma's activism overcame class-based resources reinforced by racism. The family-focused factory-hand woman made her investments close at hand and for her they worked out. Sub-marginal life that lacks the financial prerequisites for any engagement other than survival is never satisfactory. Life just above the margins, despite cumulative deprivations, can be satisfying for some who invest where they can. Especially when the family investment works out and persons do not fall into an economic sub-basement, life within limits can be meaningful. Yet, even in such conditions, there are the injuries of class.

The Hidden Injuries of Class

Two dimensions recurred in the stories we heard from our collaborators who had histories of deprivation. The first was that of life as struggle and the second a concept of social class as world-view.

Life as Struggle

Mary, again, typifies how the life journey may seem to be one struggle after another. She is a "winner," but only after coping with so many traumas and betrayals that we cannot help but marvel at her resilience. She is strong and vigorous. Somehow the blows that might have defeated another helped make her strong. Her confidence is still a bit fragile, and yet marvelous to behold. On the other hand, no one would characterize her life course as easy. There was always struggle to get by, to care for others, and to encompass the attacks on her own ego strength.

There were others who are surviving the struggle, but with a less clearcut victory. They are still on the move, coping with problems and limitations, and meeting what they see as their responsibilities. Yet, for them life is hard, a day-to-day effort to do what must be done. This is especially the case for the accepting adaptors who began with few resources and were always on the edge of losing even the bare requisites for coping. The costs are more than not having the time, energy, and other resources to launch out in new and exciting engagements. There is more than truncated self-development and personal creativity. For many, no one will ever know what they might have been under different circumstances.

Anna (chapter 3) is only one example of those who were continually depleted by what they had to do. The mother of twelve, working as a night janitor downtown with a husband who seems to be of little help and having her own health problems, she is just tired all the time. No one could be more tired than the woman who comes home from her own menial and demand-ing job to take care of grandchildren during the day. She is always on the edge of collapse with no likelihood of respite in sight.

"Life is struggle" can sound very existential. It can connote courage and strength, entering the storms of life and emerging on the other side a fuller and stronger person. But what if there is no "other side?" What if the struggle just goes on and on, demanding and unrelenting? For some, later life is such a struggle, and the resources seem to be diminishing rather than accumulating.

Class as a World-View

A second "hidden injury" is the perspective of what is defined as real and possible in life. We like to think of youth as a time of dreaming, of contem-plating the wide possibilities of the future. For some, not all, that may well be true. It certainly was not for all our sample. Some had their "youth" cut short by economic necessity. They were out of school after a very few years, not due to lack of ability, but because their families became sub-marginal. They just were not able to feed and cloth everyone.

Again, most accepting adaptors illustrate life with near horizons most fully. They are so enmeshed in the daily requirements of life that they don't tend to look much farther. "This is what life is." "God has given this life, and my duty is to cope with it." The implication is that this is all that life is. The range of possibilities that are part of the mental ecology of most just are not there. It's a "small world after all," but not in a way to sing about. For some, the same religious perspective that provides comfort also contributes to the limited world view. That there are resources to be grasped, possibilities of change to be explored, or forces to be fought just doesn't seem to come to mind. Rather, as limited as life is, that's the way it is—that and no more.

A second aspect of the same issue is found in the family-focused. Remember that they tended to have much lower education levels than the balanced investors. Many had developed satisfying lives. There was certainly an element of choice in their family investment. Yet, many of the stories suggested that no alternative had been explored. These women and men saw what was available to them, not developmental leisure or work investments but home and family. They had hopes for their children as well as a vision of how they would enter life's later periods still tied to and supported by that immediate community. Its a real world, a viable world, and yet still one with proximate horizons. It is what is available. In fact, for so many of the self-sufficients or adaptors, even that context of investment had been denied.

Class as a Life Condition

To summarize, we are presenting a somewhat different view of social class and its consequences. Without disparaging valuable research on very large samples of workers and households that requires quantitative measures of everything included, interpretive research adds some other dimensions. Social class is more than indices and variables. It is cumulative resources and deprivations through the life course. It is life as lived.

Life chances are structures of resources and opportunities. For some, it is life on the margins, an inability even to find the doorways that might lead to something better. For some, it is a journey that never seems to get started, that is trapped from the beginning. For some, it is struggle within the confines of a world with close-in dimensions. It is daily and weekly with no confidence that things will ever get any better.

Social class is not an inevitable life sentence. We remember Mary and Alma. It is not a condition without variation or without any happiness. But it is a pervasive condition that never lets up on a few real people. Growing old in America may be better than it was even 20 years ago, and it may be getting better for more and more. There remain, however, those who struggle and do not always overcome. Current rates of marital dissolution, structural layoffs for adults and massive unemployment for entry-level inner city youth, and new health threats replacing the old do not produce any confidence that the clear costs of class are just history.

References

Bendix, Reinhard, and S. Lipset, eds. 1966. *Class, Status, and Power*. New York: The Free Press.

Rubin, Lillian. 1976. *Worlds of Pain*. New York: Basic Books.

Sennett, Richard, and J. Cobb. 1973. *The Hidden Injuries of Class*. New York: Vintage Books.

Sewell, William H., and R. Hauser. 1975. *Education, Occupation, and Earnings*. New York: Academic Press.

Weber, Max. 1930. *The Protestant Ethic and the Spirit of Capitalism*. Translated by T. Parsons. New York: Charles Scribners' Sons.

10
Life's Second Half—
What is Success?

The concept of "success" in life is attended with so many complications and controversies that it might best be avoided altogether. Probably no one except a television reporter would now equate success with sheer longevity. At the same time, one would have to see life with incredible narrowness to argue that success is fully measured by any scales of self-reported life satisfaction or functional competence. From the perspective of this study, success would be related to how well our collaborators had coped with change. But, who is to judge? Are self-reports more accurate than evaluations of their stories by the research staff or analyses of widely used scales? And, is not success relative? How can we compare those who have had to cope with devastating turning points or a series of zigzagging traumas with those who have sailed through later life with comprehensive resources and only predictable transitions?

In a case study approach, the resources and strategies of each person may be assessed one by one. To do that would require another book rather than a relatively brief final chapter. Further, the deeper we go into the specificities of coping, the less are we able to draw any kinds of conclusions that might provide clues for those who will be coping with their own or others' later-life changes.

Our compromise has been to employ the typologies of the life course and of coping styles that seem to capture many of the most salient dimensions of the cases. Every difference between the styles and strategies of, for example, Nat and Mary is not defined by his being family-focused and her balanced investing. Both their resources and their problems differ as do their genders, race, and marital and occupational histories. Strategies are, however, something that can be the basis for self-assessment and for counseling. Mary is an example of someone who dealt with a series of traumas and betrayals by identifying the range of resources that she could incorporate into a total strategy of rebuilding her life. By almost any standards, she is a "success" despite the traumas and limited resources. Perhaps the typologies will help us to identify persistent elements of coping that can be taken up by those facing their own later life changes.

Life Satisfaction: An Index of Success

Probably the most commonly used measures of success are the various life satisfaction scales with their own long histories of development. In this study we used six items measuring recollective satisfaction from the most widely employed scale, the Life Satisfaction Index (Neugarten et al., 1961). This LSI scale has multiple dimensions (Liang, 1984). Our interest was concentrated on a summation of the life course as perceived by the individual. This index of general satisfaction is one way of ascertaining how people feel about the way things have gone for them.

It comes as no surprise that there are measurable differences in subjective well-being among those with different coping styles (see table 10–1). Statistically the differences were significant at the .001 level with a Cramer's V of .358 and a Lambda of .12 with satisfaction dependent.

These percentages are presented only for rough comparison purposes. Certainly only those categories with fifteen or more persons can be given any distribution credence. Even so, however, there are some interesting comparisons among those four:

> The "personal" styles of coping, the self-sufficient and accepting adaptors, have far and away the highest proportions with low life satisfaction.

> The family-focused are as satisfied as the balanced investors. This suggests that concentration on that proximate life domain provides an adequate realm for investment and source of support when it works and when the world is defined that way.

External resources and reliable social integration are better than going it alone when the possibilities are there. The parsimonious explanation of self-sufficiency was a lack of access to such relationships. The high satisfaction of the five faithful members reinforces this conclusion. In general, being detached from communities of those with whom we can share life raises the likelihood of dissatisfaction. This is consistent with decades of research employing different methods (Larson, 1978).

There seems to be no magic in either work or leisure, if we can place any reliance in those tiny numbers. Rather, both contribute most to satisfaction when they are part of an integrated style of multiple investments. There were, however, the two quite satisfied persons who had organized their life

Table 10–1
Life Satisfaction by Coping Style

Style	% High	% Medium	% Low	Row total
		Life Satisfaction		
Balanced Investors	39.6	35.4	25.0	40% (48)
Family-Focused	43.5	34.8	21.7	19% (23)
Work-Centered	50.0	0	50.0	3% (4)
Leisure-Invested	0	50.0	50.0	3% (4)
Faithful Members	40.0	60.0	0	4% (5)
Diffuse Dabblers	25.0	50.0	25.0	3% (4)
Self-Sufficient	6.7	53.3	39.9	12% (15)
Accepting Adaptors	13.3	33.3	53.3	12% (15)
Resistant Rebels	0	0	100.0	2% (2)

around work careers that offered viable identities and opportunities for development.

Multivariate analysis of life satisfaction produced much the same results. The quality of personal relationships (subjective social integration) and the level of leisure activity were the two primary factors differentiating those with high from those with low life satisfaction (Steinkamp and Kelly, unpublished paper). Further, entered first, health, marital status, age, education level, gender, and occupation level together accounted for less than 12% of the variance in life satisfaction. Controlling for all those factors, leisure added over 6% (Kelly et al. 1987). When entered independently, leisure activity level accounted for almost twice the variance of self-reported health, the next strongest factor, 13% to 7%.

Leisure, family, work, and community are significant resources for later-life coping. They have provided resources with which the well-endowed and the dispossessed, women and men, have been able to cope. Clearly it is those cut off from such resources, especially from significant other people, who have more difficulty coping with change. Further, such relationships are reciprocal: there is investment in activity and relationships as well as gaining support from them.

The Invariability of Change

Further, the life-course context of such coping is one in which change is inevitable. There is now considerable evidence that unexpected traumas are more disrupting than on-time and anticipated transitions. In fact, more often than not, the transitions of launching and retirement are anticipated positively. On the other hand, being widowed or divorced during a life period in which most associates remain in intact marriages wrenches the newly single adults out of familiar social contexts. The support of intimates in one's age cohort may be lost. The single becomes the "odd one out" and must reconstitute a viable set of those sharing similar hanges. Only some family and occasional intimate friends are still there when traumas strike "off time."

What cannot be stressed too much is that the life course is made up of change and transitions at least as much as periods of relative stability. Sixty percent of our subsample were either turning point or zigzag life-course types. That includes many who were in their 40s and 50s as well as the older cohorts. Clearly most adults have to cope with unanticipated disruptions sometime in the second half of life. Health, family, and work changes will be abrupt and require major change in order to cope. Rebuilding the framework as well as the details of life is the common, not esoteric, experience of adult living.

How Do They Make It?

Most seem to do at least reasonably well. On an 18–point life satisfaction scale, 68% had scores of 13 or higher. More important, the number who were definitively miserable was quite small. Only 14 of the 120 had scores below ten on the scale. Most of those with limited resources and major problems were at least getting by. They may not have had bright and shining futures, but they were coping and finding satisfaction in some relationships or investments. At least they found some satisfaction in the sheer fact of coping.

What does it take to make it? What are the common factors in meeting change and coming out on the other side? The answers differ for the different coping styles:

1. For the family-focused, the reliability and responsiveness of others in that immediate community are important. They are proud that their children came out all right and that they were able to make a home for them. They define their lives around this social institution and, for the most part, find it both a source of support and a realm of meaningful investment. The outcomes may not have been spectacular, but they are real and there to be experienced.

2. For the largest category, the balanced investors, the social world tends to have wider horizons. They have more options, quite significant when one fails for a time. They are able to define themselves multi-dimensionally and to experience more variety through the life course. They have more ebb and flow among life domains. Since they tend to enter adult life with greater resources, it is not surprising that they continue to invest in and receive help from a wider range of relationships and activities.

3. For the self-sufficient, the key factor seems to be a self-definition of strength and independence. Their internal resources have to be based on considerable emotional stability and a sense of inner competence.

4. For accepting adaptors, change is met with a passive absorption rather than an active response. Insofar as they are able to cope, the factors seem to be minimal social and personal resources coupled with low expectations. Those with the highest satisfaction seem to be those with a religious grounding for their acceptance.

Yet, there are two elements that are common to almost all who express satisfaction with how they had met the problems and changes of life.

The first is some kind of courage. It takes courage to act, to respond to change with change. Almost without exception, those who had rebuilt lives that they found satisfying had taken risks. Some were women who had expected to be family-centered and whose wider investments were a response to failure in that domain. They had reached out to other people and let them know their need to share. They had tried new activities, new jobs, and new social environments. They had prepared themselves for different work environments, tried new leisure, or made new friends.

Underlying such courage is some sense of self-worth. Usually one or more significant others helped by demonstrating that they believed the persons having to cope with difficulties "could do it." This sense of self-worth has a number of components in varying mixtures. There is an integrity of meaning in which one believes that all this can make sense. There is some resilience so that adaptation does not become devastating. There is a sense that one is "worth it," that even betrayals and loss do not diminish the self to the extent that there is no base on which to reconstitute a viable life. And there is a sense of competence, that one can take effectual action, no matter how limited.

The second element is community. The number of self-sufficients who really made it alone is very small, only one in the high level of satisfaction and nine in the middle level. Even they were often "helpers" who had some involvement with others. Without question, some access to reliable and responsive relationships is crucial. That is the critical difference between the family-focused and those whose coping styles are more personal. In some cases, it is not a matter of choice. But the reality of "sharing" in a time of coping with traumatic change is an irreplacable dimension of coping. Further, as already analyzed, the optimal situation is multicontextual. When only one set of social roles dominates life, then the possibilities of replacing loss in that single context are reduced. The importance of "the friend" for so many adult women suggests that there are sources of intimacy and support other than the family. Even the less communicative interaction patterns important to retirement-age men are examples of the value of a diversity of relationships. Most of us need other people with whom we share relationships of communication, trust, and caring to cope with the expected and the unexpected changes of the life course.

Personal Sources of Strength

Social sources of support have been well identified. We did not emphasize more personal or individual sources of strength in our research design. There are, however, some suggestions of such sources and resources.

The first is a series of life experiences that yield a sense of competence. Those who cope best with later-life change are those who have come to believe that they have the ability to do what is necessary. In their families, work, or play, they have developed an existential self-definition that "I am able." They believe that they are able to recreate their lives when necessary because they have demonstrated self-determination in the past.

The second source of personal strength is often a "myth", a meaningful story. Most people have no profound and articulated "philosophy of life." Even the most thoughtful tend to explain their lives in stories that are frequently punctuated by aphorisms that sound like they are out of an old almanac. Yet, there is coherence to these stories and summative statements. Most of our collaborators had some kind of myth about themselves and the meaning of their lives. They had thought about all this, just as midlife and older adults are supposed to do. Their myth might be couched in terms of roles: as parents or friends, workers or members, helpers or survivors. A few had developed myths with more of a lonely heroism theme. Many of the myths had religious overtones and some were deeply theological. But almost everyone who was at all successful in coping with life had some kind of story that made sense of it all. Rather than be disturbed that such myths distorted the "reality" of events, we believe that the myths are an integral part of the coping process.

The third source of personal strength is in motivational orientations. Most people may not be sure just where they are going in terms of outcomes. Most do, however, have a sense of direction. Their motivational patterns may be primarily affiliational as they focus on primary relationships and on nurturing and caring. They may be more oriented toward challenge and accomplishment. Or, in a few cases, they may be reaching out for a variety of experiences. The point is that those who cope with change best have some sense of motion and momentum. They are moving toward life rather than just accepting whatever comes along. There are gender differences in motivation as well as those based on past experiences and access to resources. Some orientations seem to work better than others in later life. Too much concentration on challenge and accomplishment, for example, may not mesh well with retirement. The social constrictions of frailty may be especially hard for those for whom some social position and affilation have been central. Nevertheless, it is important to have a sense of direction, an inner source of motivation to keep on the move as long and as fully as possible.

The Stories of Coping

Perhaps "coping" isn't really the right word on which to hang the stories of so many of our collaborators. Coping seems to connote just getting by. It is true that many were conventional, that some were just barely making it, and that a few were bitter and alienated. Somehow, however, the stories that seem most memorable were something more. They were stories of people with very limited resources, especially educationally and economically, who had met life's storms with courage and overcame the battering with strength and resilance. They were, as the phrase has it, knocked down but never knocked out. They had courage to an extent that provokes wonder and even awe.

There were also the stories of community and caring, family and friends who were truly "there for each other." Being available and reliable for other seldom comes without some cost to personal agendas and convenience. Sometimes "being there" is a matter of seeing no alternatives. A spouse, son, daughter, brother, or sister may say, "If I don't do it, no one will." But the point is that they were responsive and responsible. They did what was needed and usually something more. Sometimes those who were left alone had to reach out to forge new bonds, to create new relationships. Sometimes it was work or play associates, others in some institutional relationship, or just friends or neighbors who offered access to communication and support. We found few who were deeply alone, even among those who had outlived most of their persistent relationships.

Whoever said that life was easy? Certainly no one who had even a second-hand experience with our 120 later-life adults getting through the winter of later life. Limited resources, loss, hurt, and change have been known all too well by most of them. Yet, more often than not, they are making it all right. In fact, most are doing better than that in lives that do have some quiet courage and consistent community. And we have gained from their willingness to share.

References

Kelly, John R., M. Steinkamp, and J. Kelly, 1987. "Later-Life Satisfaction: Does Leisure Contribute?" *Leisure Sciences* 10:1.

Larson, R. 1978. "Thirty Years of Research on the Subjective Well-Being of Older Americans." *Journal of Gerontology* 27:511–523.

Liang, Jersey. 1984. "Dimensions of the Life Satisfaction Index A: A Structural Formulation." *Journal of Gerontology* 39:613–622.

Neugarten, Bernice L., R. Havighurst, and S. Tobin. 1961. "The Measurement of Life Satisfaction." *Journal of Gerontology* 16:134–143.

Steinkamp, Marjorie, and J. Kelly. 1986. "Social Integration, Leisure Activity, and Life Satisfaction among Older Adults." Unpublished paper.

Index

About the Author

John R. Kelly is a professor in the department of leisure studies and the Institute for Research on Human Development at the University of Illinois at Urbana-Champaign. He received the Ph.D. in sociology in 1972 from the University of Oregon and master's degrees from Yale, Oregon, and the University of Southern California. His previous books are *Freedom to Be: a New Sociology of Leisure* (1987), *Recreation Business* (1986), *Leisure Identities and Interactions* (1983), and *Leisure* (1982). His research on adult life-course changes and styles has been supported by the National Institute on Aging and other agencies. He was born in Chicago in 1930 and has taught in Oregon, Wisconsin, Virginia, and Illinois.